HOW TO LENGTHEN YOUR STRIDE *Without* GETTING A HERNIA

HOW TO LENGTHEN YOUR STRIDE *Without* GETTING A HERNIA

K. DOUGLAS BASSETT

CFI
Springville, Utah

ISBN 13: 978-1-59955-291-0

Published by CFI, an imprint of Cedar Fort, Inc., 2373 W. 700 S., Springville, UT 84663
Distributed by Cedar Fort, Inc. www.cedarfort.com

LIBRARY OF CONGRESS CATALOGING-IN-PUBLICATION DATA

Bassett, Doug.
How to lengthen your stride : without getting a hernia / K. Douglas Bassett.
p. cm.
ISBN 978-1-59955-291-0 (acid-free paper)
1. Christian life--Mormon authors. I. Title.

BX8656.B38 2009
248.4'89332--dc22

2009008935

Cover design by Angela D. Olsen
Cover design © 2009 by Lyle Mortimer
Edited and typeset by Melissa J. Caldwell

Printed in the United States of America

10 9 8 7 6 5 4 3 2 1

Printed on acid-free paper

To my sweet wife, Arlene
Loving her has been the easiest thing I've ever done

acknowledgments

I am grateful to Vern, ReNae, and Lisa Christensen whose work with the rough draft was invaluable.

It has been blessing to work with my friends at Cedar Fort, Inc. I am particularly grateful to Melissa Caldwell for her editing skills. Also, Jennifer Fielding for her encouragement during the development for the manuscript and Angela Olsen for her work on the cover design.

My heartfelt thanks goes out to Rob Beatty and Jacob Jorgenson for their singular contributions to this book.

I am so grateful beyond expression for my magnificent eternal companion, Arlene, and my entire family for their patience and timely suggestions regarding the text. Also, my brother Dennis for his valuable assistance in establishing the flow of the first few chapters.

Finally, I acknowledge my Heavenly Father's hand in anything of lasting value connected with this book.

Contents

Preface ix

1. Fear 1

2. Conquering Fear 19

3. Anger and the Unforgiving Heart 39

4. Optimism 57

5. Gratitude 83

6. Finding Peace in a World of Conflict 96

7. Lengthen Your Stride without Getting a Hernia 115

About the Author 134

Preface

Have you ever felt like you could not find the energy to move forward? Years ago, as a married graduate student with seven children, I woke up one Sunday morning with the thought, "I am just overwhelmed; I don't think I'm going to church today."

I rationalized, "After all, isn't Sunday a day of rest? I'm going to stay home and rest."

However, as I reviewed my responsibilities, I didn't feel I could place my duties on someone else at the last minute. The more responsible side of me reminded, "You can delegate authority, but you can't delegate responsibility."

So with that mini-lecture I went to church with the feeling that my present circumstances had me so overloaded that I didn't have the strength to carry it much further. Everything that was on my shoulders seemed to weigh on me like a load of hay—my back was telling me that it couldn't take one more piece of straw.

As I sat on the stand looking at my family, I was grateful for my decision to be where I should be. Halfway through the meeting a stake representative stood at the pulpit. Like a coach giving a halftime speech to a team that had been playing terrible, he reminded us that we were not doing enough to build the kingdom. The more he spoke the more overwhelmed I felt. He was a wonderful man with a wonderful message, but in my present mind-set, it felt like that last straw was being placed on my back.

He concluded his message by reminding us to "lengthen our stride." When he sat down, the thought came to me, "How do I lengthen my stride when I'm having a hernia?"

As I moved forward with faith, I found the words of President Thomas S. Monson to be true: "When we are on the Lord's errand, we are entitled to the Lord's help. Remember that the Lord will shape the back to bear the burden placed upon it."[1]

Over the years, I have discovered that it is not uncommon for people in the Church to feel what I did on that Sunday. Some even carry it for an extended period of time. I believe that life is filled with defining moments. That Sunday morning was certainly one for me. Those moments often come when we are face-to-face with a negative attitude or disposition, which will beat us down if we embrace it. Often, it is a battle that must be fought on a daily basis, over an extended period of time. This book is my effort to aid the reader in dealing with those defining moments when it is required of us to step forward with our best selves—to embrace the finest that is in us.

Has the fear of failure ever washed over you like a dark wave?

Do you find that other people's opinions of you have more power than they should?

Have you ever been so discouraged, it was hard to complete even the simplest of tasks?

Would you like to have the ability to believe that "everything will work out"?

Is it hard to accept that people are basically good?

Do you find it difficult to express gratitude?

Have you discovered that your tendency to laugh has diminished as you have gotten older?

Is anger an emotional option you would like to overcome?

Is it hard not to live in the past?

Have you struggled with the power to forgive?

Does the pace of your life seem to be out of control?

Do national and global events weigh you down to the point of losing hope?

This book is my attempt at dealing with these questions as well as others that we face in this world we share.

Notes

1. Thomas S. Monson, "To Learn, To Do, To Be," *Ensign*, May 1992, 48.

chapter one

Fear

As an undersized third grader in the small town of Gridley, California, I dutifully headed for the bus after another long day of summer school. I headed approximately in the direction of the big yellow school bus like a lone sheep meandering aimlessly without a shepherd. I wasn't too thrilled about school in general, but I was totally "underwhelmed" with the prospect of education during the hot summer months when my friends were swimming, playing baseball, and doing just about anything that would be more fun than sitting in a classroom.

Resembling a condemned man, I trudged along with my head down in a bored trance, my eyes seeing only enough to keep me from falling over. Barely conscious, I progressed across the grass field that was used during the day for football, softball, soccer, and track.

My pity party came to an abrupt halt when my eyes caught hold of something I had never viewed before. A group of boys a few years older than me were jumping over a thin hollow bar balanced precariously about four feet off the ground and on top of two adjustable standers about ten feet apart. After sailing up and over the elongated obstacle, they victoriously landed in a pile of sawdust. It was the first thing I had seen all day that looked inviting.

The destination of the school bus was instantly forgotten as my mind, body, and soul gravitated toward the high jump pit. All of the afternoon's obligations and agreements were forgotten as I focused on that activity like metal to a magnet. Caught up in the excitement, I lost sight of the age difference between me and the participants, and the unwritten rules of conversation connected to that disparity.

"I think I can do that!" I exclaimed.

The fellow who seemed to be at the head of the pecking order looked in my direction. I suppose the fact that he was the biggest and best athlete in the group made him the natural spokesman. "Even if you could," he said condescendingly, "we wouldn't let you."

My youthful enthusiasm got the best of my social inhibitions, and without hesitation, I said, "I really think I can jump over that bar."

With a mock wave of his hand in the direction of the high jump pit, he sent out an invitation for failure, "Be my guest."

It was obvious that none of the boys thought I had a chance of clearing the bar. If I had given it much thought I probably would have felt the same. With an exuberance completely founded in the ignorance of youth, I dropped my backpack and jogged toward the front of the high jump pit. Measuring my approach, I jumped up at the last moment and threw myself over the bar. To my surprise, the older boys cheered as they approached the sawdust to congratulate me. Like the underdog who bloodies the bully's nose, I was part of the group only because I had the natural talent to do something that was of value to those boys. In that sense I was one of them, but because of our age difference, I immediately played the role of the mascot. After all, you can't totally include someone who is the age of your younger brother. What kind of message would that send younger brothers?

The next day I was part of the track team. I started competing and winning and just having fun. I expected to win because I was too young and inexperienced with life to see it any other way. I discovered that my continued success shortened the distance caused by the age gap between me and those I competed against. But I was having too much fun to pay much attention to the social rewards of winning.

A year or so later, my family moved to Fresno, California, and by age twelve I was a part of the Sierra Foothill Track Team. This private club was made up of specially selected athletes representing the Fresno area. Perhaps the greatest bonus was the fact that from time to time I received instruction from Bob Mathias, the gold medal winner in the decathlon in the 1948 Helsinki and 1952 London Summer Olympic Games. From age twelve to fourteen, I was able to compete in the best stadiums from Fresno to Los Angeles in front of thousands of spectators. It was quite a heady atmosphere for a young boy to grow up in.

Suddenly, this path hit a detour when my family moved to Yuba City,

Doug Bassett with Olympic champion Bob Mathias

California. However, it wasn't long before I started getting attention once again because of my leaping ability. By the time I approached high school age, it was only natural that I would be on the track team. Track didn't seem like such a big deal to me because the large stadiums filled with thousands of fans in southern California had been replaced with small high school fields smattered with supporting parents and family members in this northern California agricultural area. It was still fun because of my association with the other members of the team and, frankly, because winning had become a habit by this point. I participated because it came natural and it seemed I had always done it.

But though I enjoyed track, my heart was truly in another arena—basketball. My hero was a Spanish player on the varsity basketball team named Robert Ortiz. Before the days of the three point shot he would park himself so far from the hoop that few would think to guard him. It seemed that every game the opposition would leave him alone in disbelief, thinking that no one would dare attempt a two point shot from that far out. Game after game he proved them wrong as he bombed in shots from what seemed like the parking lot.

As I practiced my shots, I would do everything I could to be like my hero. The small basketball court in my backyard was the stage where I played the role of Robert Ortiz. Alone in my world, my voice could be heard by the birds in the trees as both the announcer and the roaring crowd. In those hours my fantasy was almost real. During the day I was just me, an undersized insecure freshman high jumper, but in my spare time, I was Robert Ortiz.

One afternoon, without warning, as I was practicing at the school high jump pit, my world changed. The routine that day was the same as it had been for years—jump over the bar and return and do it again and again. It had become a habit, like putting on my socks. It seemed as natural as breathing. Nothing analytical—just do it. My workout involved no time in the weight room or anything else, which would be common for today's athletes.

Suddenly, the calmness was interrupted with these words, "You're him, aren't cha!"

I turned in the direction of the source to hear once again, "You're him—you're the guy!"

I couldn't believe it. These words were coming from Robert Ortiz. He motioned for me to join him next to the high jump bar. With one hand on my shoulder he pointed to the bar and spoke as calmly as if he were describing a warm summer's day. "Look at you! You're built like a drowned rat. You don't appear to have a muscle on your body. You don't even look like an athlete."

His words hit me like a sucker punch. Coming from someone else the expression wouldn't have meant much, but from the mouth of my hero, they went straight to my heart. In truth, they went straight to my soul—they just pierced my heart on their way through.

With no thought of offending, he continued, "Answer a question for me, would you? How do you get such a skinny little body over a bar so far over your head?"

The stunned look on my face bore witness to the fact that a reply would not be soon in coming.

Undeterred, Robert pressed forward, "I really want to know how you do it. It's impossible, but you do it." My silence was broken with a slight punch to the shoulder and a "sentence sermon" from my hero. "Good for you."

His last words of encouragement may be best categorized as "too little too late."

I stood there in silence. It was as if the bird of paradise had flown into my life and deposited an unexpected gift on my shoulder. I didn't have the strength to wipe it off.

He turned on his heels, leaving the scene of emotional carnage totally unaware of what was happening inside of me. I really believe he was trying to pay me a compliment. That may have been true intellectually, but his words left me deflated emotionally. It was as if I was being congratulated for being the homecoming queen and then asked how someone so ugly could obtain such an honor.

Even after he had walked into the distance, his words remained, silently festering like a cancer in my heart. I turned and faced the bar looming in front of the high jump pit. His words resonated within me. "How do I get this skinny body over that bar? It's impossible but I do it. How do I do it? It is impossible, it is impossible!"

For the first time I introduced into my heart the possibility—no, the probability—of failure. I stepped back and attempted to jump over the bar. I slammed into the bar; I felt a pain in my knee I had never experienced. I got up and repeated the procedure as I had done a thousand times before. But this time the results were different because I was different. My heart had been changed. I had lost faith in myself. The words of someone respected had been digested in the heart of an insecure boy, and what had been fun because of the expectation of success had been changed as quickly as belief to unbelief. At an older season in my life, there would have been no negative fallout. But at that age, at that time, with those words coming from one so revered, the results were extreme.

That was it; I walked away from the high jump pit with the excuse of a sore knee. One day's missed practice turned into two, which turned into a week, then a month, and I never went back. I quit believing in my ability to clear the bar, and that, which had come as natural as taking my next breath, no longer held the same appeal. Without warning, a chapter of my life had ended as quietly as turning a page, simply because in the arena of high jumping a boy stopped having faith in his abilities. When my mind believed fully that I could fly over the high jump bar, my body completed the journey. When I stopped believing, it was only natural for my body to follow the map laid out by my thoughts.

It now seems odd to me, but I went over twenty years without even thinking of that story. I just put it out of my mind and moved on. As a teacher, I am constantly looking for those things in life that allow me to connect with and lift my students. One day, as I was preparing a lesson, my thoughts stumbled through my youth and found that story. It's interesting how time and maturity allowed me to focus on the experience with the warmth and fondness of reminiscing over an old photograph. I was able to view the event as a learning experience, with no regrets—grateful to be able to capitalize on life's lessons. As I measured the impact of one conversation with Robert Ortiz, it reminded me of the power of the words I have used over the years with young people. As a parent, grandparent, and teacher, I can't be reminded of that enough.

I have discovered in decades of teaching and counseling that my high jumping story is not unique. The tragedy is not that my hero's negative words were spoken but that the negative words were believed. Life is filled with input from many different sources. Some of the most successful people I know have come through some extremely harsh circumstances and the negative input that accompanied them. The difference was they refused to digest it. They chose a higher mental path and the positive input that accompanied it. In the final analysis, discouragement doesn't keep regular hours. Doubting yourself becomes the gift that keeps on giving. This is true of all negative emotions, such as the fear of failure, worry, anxiety, stress, and so on. This certainly was the case with my high jumping career.

I'm convinced that when our lives are placed in review, the vast majority of life's "defining decisions" will be connected to two polar opposites—our deepest fears and our most passionate faith.

When we make decisions from the perspective of fear, we are running from something. In a sense we are making decisions by default—circumstance is making the decision for us. Fearful decisions are tied more to our emotions than to our intellect. They require no logic at all—like when I quit high jumping. That is why we can look back over time at these moments and say, "I know what I was feeling, but what was I thinking?" In truth, we were thinking very little. We were reacting—like the reflex of ducking from a fist that is suddenly headed in our direction. Our minds are paralyzed when our hearts are filled with fear. That is why we can make fearful decisions without thinking things through. The decisions we make under the duress of fear, we often make to escape an "unpleasant present." The motive is to close doors on the "negative now" rather than open doors to a "positive future."

Whereas, when we make decisions from the perspective of passionate faith, we run toward something. What we feel is not fear of something negative but a hunger to move in the direction of something positive. Faith often give us time to think things through—like the decision to be baptized or the decision to marry in the temple. And when our faith is based upon truth, time only reinforces that we did the right thing. Unlike fearful decisions, faithful decisions seldom require luck. It is easy to see how these contrasting viewpoints carried out over a period of time become a defining ingredient between a successful life and a life filled with failure. In truth, our entire lives are a combination of fear and faith, battling at the same time. It is our faith that allows us to win the internal battles we are waging with our fears.

I would ask you the reader to take a glance at your life up to this point and see if this is not the case. For adults within the Church, as we look only at the defining decisions of mission, marriage, and career, it is easy to see how our fears in combination with our faith have directed us on the path which has become our lives. In essence, we are shackled by our fears or liberated by the confidence that comes from what we passionately believe in. And if what we believe is true, our liberation to succeed is added upon as time goes by.

The Power of Our Fearful Thoughts

Dr. Stephen R. Covey wrote, "Most of us think we see the world as it is, but I believe this is not the case. We each see not with the eye but with the soul. Each person sees the world not as it is but as he or she is. When he opens his mouth to describe what he sees, he in effect describes himself."[1] Think of the ramifications of this truth in terms of our everyday health and happiness, as well as the long term decisions of marriage and career and so on.

Many years ago Harold Sherman wrote:

> Its human nature to feel, when something unhappy has happened, then it may happen again. Your fear of it may cause you to picture the possibility of its recurrence and, without realizing it, you have set forces in motion to attract similar conditions to you. Then when face to face with another unpleasant experience, you testify to the fact that you have anticipated it, have even helped create it by saying, "You might know this would happen to me!". . .
>
> There is a great law of mind by which your thinking and your conduct should always be guided: "Like attracts like."
>
> Think good thoughts; you will eventually attract good things. Think bad thoughts, you will ultimately attract bad [things]. . . .
>
> The surest way in the world to attract trouble is to picture the possibility of more trouble coming to you![2]

Over the years I have had the privilege of teaching at three different colleges. I have observed something that is consistent in every semester I have taught. At the beginning of the term, the students are filled with a vibrant hope, a freshness which makes the learning process in the classroom much easier. Their abundant energy is reflective of youthful exuberance. But, as the semester wears on, with all the factors of college life (not the least of which is facing the rigors of finals and papers), something predictable happens. For those students who have procrastinated, or for whatever reason have not been equal to the task, an observable change in their countenances occurs. It is obvious that even the physical health of many of these students is being tested as the term wears on. For those students who become truly ill, it is my observation that anxiety, worry, stress, and the fear of failure are major contributing factors. In fact, the only students who do not seem affected are those who end the term with the same expectation of hope and success that they possessed at the beginning of the semester.

Elder Jeffrey R. Holland echoed a similar sentiment regarding the thoughts of the youth in the Church: "I know of nothing that Satan uses quite so cunningly or cleverly in his work on a young man or woman. I speak of doubt (especially self-doubt), of discouragement, and of despair."[3]

I'm convinced that this change I see in my students is a microcosm of each of us throughout the course of our lives. Negative thoughts and emotions have a tremendous effect on our ability to perform, as well as our general well-being.

Dr. Harriet Lerner wrote,

> When we're too anxious we won't be able to gather new information, think clearly . . . , and find creative solutions. . . . And fear can run amok, flooding our system with adrenaline and hijacking our neo-cortex—the thinking part of the brain. Usually, anxiety is a mean trickster. It . . . turns your brain to oatmeal. . . . It can dig a big negative groove in your brain and make it impossible for you to hang on to a positive thought for more than five seconds. It can affect your body in ways that can feel crippling.[4]

This concept is certainly not new. Nearly six decades earlier, Harry Emerson Fosdick wrote:

> Fear is one of the most indispensable elements in the human makeup. [But] when it becomes terror, panic, [or] chronic anxiety, it is shattering. . . . Fear is every animal's elemental alarm-system, so sensitively keyed that at the first sign of danger the organism snaps into readiness for flight or fight. . . . The adrenal glands . . . furnish us in every frightening situation with "a swig of our own internal fight-tonic." A little of it—even in the proportion of one part to one million parts of water—is stimulating; too much of it is poison. . . . All fear is thus an alarm, in response to which the adrenal glands spring into action and the tragedy of habitual anxiety and dread is that they constitute a continuous false alarm, repeatedly calling out the fire department when there is no fire, turning the invaluable adrenal secretion, epinephrine, from an emergency stimulant into a chronic poison. . . . Fear in all its forms has a direct physical effect. . . . Anxious fear . . . always involves the misuse of the imagination. . . . The curse of fear is that it gets itself taken too seriously."[5]

The Deadly Effects of Fear

When we gaze into the crib of a baby that is well taken care of and secure, we will see something unique to the very young. If we look carefully into his eyes, he seems to have the notion that the whole world is out to do him good. Sadly, for each of us a time comes in our lives when we realize that this notion, as it relates to the "entire world," is not true. It seems to come much earlier into the life of a young person today than it used to, since the world has become more dangerous and families less secure. Statements such as "Seventy percent of all patients who come to physicians could cure themselves if they only got rid of their fears and worries," and "Fear, worry, hate, supreme selfishness, and the inability to adjust . . . to the world of reality . . . were largely the causes of . . . stomach illnesses" remind us that we must mature emotionally if we are to deal with life profitably in the real world.[6]

Even LDS Church history is filled with similar examples. In many instances, emotional well-being had a direct correlation to the physical health of the individual. Many years ago, President Spencer W. Kimball "felt sick and asked Dr. [Russell M.] Nelson to check him over. The doctor found nothing physically wrong, yet Spencer was visibly distressed. Probing, Dr. Nelson learned that Spencer had received news that two missionaries in Texas had been murdered and dismembered by a mentally disturbed man. *Spencer's concern for the families of the missionaries made him literally ill.*"[7]

A wise man once said:

> You do not get stomach ulcers from what you eat. You get ulcers from what is eating you. . . . Worry can make even the most stolid person ill. General [Ulysses S.] Grant discovered that during the closing days of the Civil War. . . . Grant had been besieging Richmond for nine months. General Lee's troops, ragged and hungry, were beaten. Entire regiments were deserting at a time. . . . Grant was in hot pursuit, banging away at the Confederates from both sides and the rear. . . . Grant, half blind with a violent sick headache, fell behind his army and stopped at a farmhouse.
>
> "I spent the night," he records in his Memoirs, "in bathing my feet in hot water and mustard, and putting mustard plasters on my wrists and back part of my neck, hoping to be cured by morning."
>
> The next morning, he was cured instantaneously. And the thing that cured him was not a mustard plaster, but a horseman galloping down the road with a letter from Lee, saying he wanted to surrender.
>
> "When the officer [bearing the message] reached me," Grant wrote, "I was still suffering with the sick headache, but the instant I saw the contents of the note, I was cured."
>
> *Obviously it was Grant's worries, tensions, and emotions that made him ill. He was cured instantly the moment his emotions took on the hue of confidence, achievement, and victory.*[8]

President Gordon B. Hinckley said, "Let us recognize that fear comes not of God, but rather that this gnawing, destructive element comes from the adversary of truth and righteousness. Fear is the antithesis of faith. It is corrosive in its effects, *even deadly*."[9]

When I first read this statement by President Hinckley, I became fascinated by his use of the word "deadly." As I have researched his hypothesis, I am convinced he is absolutely right. Our thoughts have the power to effect the very health of our bodies, even to the point of squeezing our lives from us. Norman Vincent Peale bore witness to this squeezing when he declared, "You were not born with the worry habit. You acquired it. Worry . . . is derived from an old Anglo-Saxon word meaning 'to choke.' If someone were to put his fingers around your throat and press hard, cutting off the flow of vital power, it would be a dramatic demonstration of what you do to yourself by long-held and habitual worry."[10] *Worry* is so closely related to *fear* that at times they are used as synonyms.

President Hinckley's sentiments regarding the deadly effects of negative emotions are echoed by the Prophet Mormon in a letter to his son Moroni: "My son, . . . may not the things which I have written grieve thee, to *weigh thee down unto death*" (Moroni 9:25, italics added).

Over fifty years ago at the Harvard Medical School, the deadly effects of negative emotions such as fear, worry, and stress on our physical bodies were manifested. A middle aged woman with low-grade congestive heart failure was in the clinic for a regular checkup. The visit was nothing out of the ordinary until the professor of cardiology, Dr. Levine, a well-respected physician, entered the clinic. His rapport with everyone connected to the clinic was exceptional. He had been working with this particular patient for over a decade. He was followed by a large entourage of visiting physicians. His greeting to the patient was warmly presented and welcomed by the patient. Turning to his entourage, he said, "This woman has TS." Within moments of the observation he exited the clinic.

Immediately, the patient showed symptoms that were quite alarming. She became anxious and fearful and took breaths that clearly indicated she was hyperventilating. She began perspiring heavily and her pulse rose to over 150 beats per minute. Her lungs, which had been clear a few minutes earlier, were now developing moist crackles at the base.

The attending physician inquired of the patient as to the sudden change in her demeanor. She replied, "Dr. Levine said that I had TS, which I know stands for Terminal Situation."

Even when she was told that *TS* meant "tricuspid stenosis," she would not believe it unless it came from the mouth of Dr. Levine. The problem was enhanced by the fact that he was nowhere to be found. This story may have had a different ending in this day of cell phones and pagers, but that was not the case. As the day progressed her condition continued to worsen. Even with all the energies of the medical professionals, later in the afternoon she died of heart failure.[11]

Dr. Levine didn't cause her death any more than Robert Ortiz killed my high jumping career. But when we digest certain beliefs about ourselves, our world naturally begins to conform. Even the body seems to react in amazing ways. Fortunately, for me it was only a physical performance; for this middle-aged librarian the results were fatal. Over time, our world begins to conform to our self-perception.

The Prophet Joseph Smith's mother related the following:

> Jason, my oldest brother, . . . formed an acquaintance with a young woman of wealthy parentage. She was the pride of the place in which she resided, . . . Jason became deeply in love with her, insomuch that his heart was completely hers, and it would have been as easy to have convinced him that he could exist without his head as that he could live and enjoy life without being united with her in marriage. These feelings, I believe, were mutual, and Jason and she entered into an engagement to be married, but, as they were making arrangements for the solemnization of their nuptials, my father received a letter from Liverpool containing information that a large amount of money was collected for him and that it was ready for his reception.
>
> On account of this intelligence it was agreed that the marriage of my brother, as my father desired that he should accompany him to Liverpool, should be deferred until their return. Accordingly, my brother left his affianced bride with a heavy heart and with this promise that he would write to her . . . at least once in three months during his absence. In three months after his departure, according to agreement, a letter arrived which indeed met with a very warm reception, but it was never followed by another from him. A young man, who kept the post office where she received her letters, formed in his heart a determination to thwart my brother, if possible, in his matrimonial prospects in order to obtain the prize himself. He commenced by using the most persuasive arguments against her marrying my brother; but not succeeding in this, he next detained his letters, and then reproached him for neglecting her. Being still unsuccessful, he forged letters purporting to be from a friend of Jason who stated that he (Jason Mack) was dead, and his friends might cease to expect him. He then urged his suit again,

> but she still rejected him and continued to do so until within four months of Jason's return, when she concluded that she had wronged the young man and that he was really more worthy than she had expected. The time also which Jason was to be absent having expired without his return, she believed that the reports concerning his death must be true. So she accepted the hand of this young man and they were united in the bonds of matrimony.
>
> As soon as Jason arrived he repaired immediately to her father's house. When he arrived there she was gone to her brother's funeral; he went in and seated himself in the same room where he had once paid his addresses to her. In a short time she came home; when she first saw him she did not know him, but when she got a full view of his countenance she recognized him and instantly fainted. From this time forward she never recovered her health, but, lingering for two years, died the *victim of disappointment.*[12]

These words from the Prophet's mother resonate through the years, "died the victim of disappointment." What an amazing epitaph!

Men in Bear Suits

Let me illustrate this truth with an old joke and connected story. A man was following his daily routine of an early morning walk in the mountains. This fellow happened to be an atheist. As he was enjoying his exercise in nature he came face to face with a furious bear. Immediately, he cried out in desperation, "Oh, God, save me!"

Instantly, he recognized the dilemma of praying to a God he felt was not in existence. With no time to spare, he edited his heavenly appeal: "If there is a God, please change this bear into a believer."

No sooner than the prayer left his lips, the bear fell to its knees and with bowed head reverently said, "Oh, Lord, for this meal I'm about to partake, I give thee thanks."

Now, here's a twist on this joke for the sake of illustration. Immediately, the man began to run for his life in the opposite direction. With the magical effects of adrenalin, he narrowly escaped becoming the main course in the bear's early morning routine. He ran to a friend's cabin where he breathlessly recounted his harrowing experience. After a while he declared with a determined will that he would not let this random encounter stand in the way of the morning ritual that had brought him so much joy. He planned to continue his morning routine as if nothing had happened.

These two men had a long running relationship, which took practical joking to the extreme. His buddy saw the opportunity to play what he felt was the perfect trick on his friend. Later in the day, with sadistic anticipation, the friend went to a costume shop in town and rented a very realistic bear suit. The following morning, he hid behind a tree in the area of the previous day's encounter. Sure enough, the man was seen in the distance heading his direction on the trail. The friend was careful to note that the man had no weapons, which would definitely alter the outcome of the trick.

The victim was about to discover that the previous day's bad luck could be repeated. With perfect timing his friendly adversary waited till the last moment and jumped from behind the tree onto the path. The man immediately locked into a "fight or flight" mode—choosing flight as the correct option. He may have even beat his personal best sprint time set the day before. In short order, the trickster pulled off the head of the bear suit and shouted to his frightened friend. Within a moment the two were involved in a strange verbal jousting of "I got you good," and "I'll find a way to get you back," which was typical of their relationship.

The "internal swig of adrenaline" that raced through the system of the man on the trail was the same on both days. The first day it saved his life, and the second day it was a waste of energy and a drain to his body; "an unnecessary jolt to the system."

If this pattern of "fight or flight" were repeated over an extended period of time, the results (as stated by President Hinckley) could be deadly. Just like in the story related by Lucy Mack Smith, the negative emotions of doubt, discouragement, despair, worry, stress, habitual terror, panic, and anxiety send a death sentence to the person thus afflicted. Misery can be the vehicle that carries the poor soul to an early end of his earthly journey.

For me personally, day-to-day stress seems to be connected to the simple truth that I would rather be somewhere else. Present moments are not my friends. My health—good and bad—directly connects to how I deal emotionally with my present moments.

I believe that one of the great victories achieved by those who are well-rounded is that they have obtained the maturity to discern the difference between the real bears of life and the men in bear suits, thus minimizing the negative baggage that weigh down so many of life's travelers.

A few years ago, I was teaching this concept to a university class. I could see that one young man seemed to be struggling with his emotions a bit. I didn't think much about it until the end of the semester when he came to my office and gave me a four inch solid candy bear as a present. As he presented me with the gift, he declared, "The past few weeks I have been ripping off the heads of many of the bear suits that have been standing in my path." He continued, "I feel the light coming back into my life."

In fact, I would go as far as declaring that when we symbolically rip the head off the bear suit we discover that we are the person inside the suit. In other words, men in bear suits are a creation of our own minds—they are nothing more than a misuse of imagination.

The Book of Mormon and Bear Suits

The Book of Mormon gives ample evidence that fear, doubt, discouragement, stress, worry, and so on, must be confronted if we are to progress in mortality. We correctly use the sons of Mosiah as great examples of faithful success in the mission field. Their fourteen plus years as full-time missionaries are an inspiration to anyone who has labored in the vineyard. Even these great servants had an inward struggle, which is common among many missionaries. Ammon declared, "When our hearts were depressed, and we were about to turn back, behold, the Lord comforted us, and said: Go amongst thy brethren, the Lamanites, and bear with patience thine afflictions, and I will give unto you success" (Alma 26:27). (Notice, the Lord is connected to the solution.)

Negative emotions are normal; it is how we respond to them that defines us. The Book of Mormon shows beyond a doubt that the Lord can perform miracles, even in the lives of missionaries who are depressed and about to turn back.

The Prophet Alma preached the gospel to the people of Ammonihah. The result? They "withstood all his words, and reviled him, and spit upon him, and caused that he should be cast out of their city" (Alma 8:13).

It is not hard to picture Alma's discouragement as he was walking away from the city, "being weighed down with sorrow, wading through much tribulation and anguish of soul" (Alma 8:14). If Alma was singing, I can picture him singing the blues. Downcast and troubled, Alma cannot be blamed if the thought crossed his mind that things couldn't get any worse. Then the angel, who many years earlier (see Alma 36:10) had rendered him speechless, appeared to him. If I were Alma, I may have thought, "Perhaps I was wrong; things could get worse."

This time the angel had a different message: "Blessed art thou, Alma; therefore, lift up thy head and rejoice, for thou hast great cause to rejoice; for thou hast been faithful in keeping the commandments of God" (Alma 8:15).

The obvious application to today's discouraged missionary is that the number of baptisms is not the measure of success, but rather by keeping the commandments even when our hearts are filled with discouragement. The angel's message to Alma is proof that the heavens rejoice when a discouraged missionary is steadfast in keeping the commandments. It is easy to be obedient when everything is going great in the mission field. But when we don't break the mission rules, even when our hearts are broken, and failure is our closest companion, perhaps the Holy Ghost is whispering the same message as the angel did to Alma, "Lift up thy head and rejoice, . . . for thou hast been faithful in keeping the commandments of God."

At this point the angel asked Alma to do the thing that may have required him to stand face-to-face with his personal bear on the path: "I am sent to command thee that thou return to the city of Ammonihah" (Alma 8:16).

It would be hard to imagine anyone being thrilled to return to a place where he had been "reviled, spit on, and cast out." We get a glimpse at how Alma faced his fears as the record shows that "he returned speedily to . . . Ammonihah" (Alma 8:18). It is so hard to return to a place that has caused us great pain. I would submit that if Alma were like many people, if he had not returned speedily but had stopped to take counsel with his fears, he may not have returned at all. However, he discovered that with the Lord's help even real bears can be conquered. And to show that Alma was not reckless in his obedience, "he entered the city by another way" (Alma 8:18).

I believe this story illustrates that we can achieve one of life's greatest victories when we keep the commandments in the midst of discouragement, fear, loneliness, and negative emotions.

In regard to facing our personal demons, Eleanor Roosevelt said, "You gain strength, courage, and confidence by every experience in which you really. . . look fear in the face. You must do the thing which you think you cannot do."[13] If this story happened today, Alma may have been encouraged to get in touch with his fears through extensive counseling before he would risk such an emotionally trying challenge. By stating this I don't mean to imply that there is no place for counseling, but with experience, which includes a degree in Psychology and thirty years as a teacher, I have noticed a trend within our culture that I believe is not in our own best interest.

Elder Boyd K. Packer identified this concern:

> We are indoctrinated that somehow we should always be instantly emotionally comfortable. When that is not so, some become anxious—and all too frequently seek relief from counseling, from analysis, and even from medication. It was meant to be that life would be a challenge. To suffer some anxiety, some depression, some disappointment, even some failure is normal. Teach our members that if they have a good, miserable day once in a while, or several in a row, to stand steady and face them. Things will straighten out.[14]

On another occasion this same Apostle stated, "We know that some anxiety and depression is caused by physical disorders, but much (perhaps most) of it is not pain of the body but of the spirit."[15]

Without any disrespect for those who genuinely need counseling or even medication, the message of this book is directed to this majority identified by Elder Packer.

Notes

1. Stephen R. Covey, *The Divine Center* (Salt Lake City: Bookcraft, 1982), 3.
2. Harold Sherman, *A Treasury of Success Unlimited,* ed. Og Mandino (New York City: Simon & Schuster, 1955), 132–133.
3. Jeffrey R. Holland, *However Long and Hard the Road* (Salt Lake City: Deseret Book, 1985), 1.
4. Harriet Lerner, *Fear and Other Uninvited Guests* (New York: Harper Collins, 2004), 54–58.
5. Harry Emerson Fosdick, *On Being a Real Person* (New York and London: Harper and Brothers, 1943), 109–132.
6. See Dale Carnegie, *How to Stop Worrying and Start Living* (New York: Simon and Schuster, 1950), 22)
7. Edward L. Kimball, *Lengthen Your Stride* (Salt Lake City: Deseret Book, 2005), 47; italics added.
8. Carnegie, *How To Stop Worrying and Start Living,* 22, 25; italics added.
9. Gordon B. Hinckley, *Teachings of Gordon B. Hinckley* (Salt Lake City: Deseret Book, 1997), 220; italics added)

10. Norman Vincent Peale, *The Power of Positive Thinking* (New York: Fawcett Crest Book, 1952), 122–26.
11. See Norman Cousins, *The Healing Heart* (New York,: Avon Books, 1983), 13–14.
12. Lucy Mack Smith, *History of Joseph Smith By His Mother, Lucy Mack Smith*, (Salt Lake City, Utah: Bookcraft, 1958), 9-11; italics added.
13. Karen McAuley, *Eleanor Roosevelt* (New York: Chelsea House Publishers, 1987), 105.
14. Boyd K. Packer, in Conference Report, April 1978, 139–40.
15. Boyd K. Packer, "The Touch of the Master's Hand," *Ensign*, May 2001, 23.

chapter two

Conquering Fear

It is much easier to identify the problem than to offer a solution. I would like to offer four areas that will lead a person away from that paralyzing shadow categorized in the first chapter as fear. I recognize that the emotions identified as worry, anxiety, and despair each deserve separate consideration. However, for my purposes in this book, I have placed them under the general category of fear. The following four solutions to fear are not meant to be all encompassing, but I believe they will empower the reader with real hope to deal with the problem.

I. Perfect Love

While serving as a missionary in England, I became friends with an elder who had a profound effect on me regarding the way I view other people. As a new zone leader, I had not yet met Elder Jarvis, but I had heard about his effectiveness for months. While his ability to lead others to Christ was legendary, the word through the grapevine was that he hadn't even learned the missionary discussions yet. (This was the era that missionaries were required to memorize the standard discussions.)

I had heard from a few of his companions that he was a gentle, hard-working missionary. Though he had been a wrestling champion in Arizona prior to his mission, he had not developed enough academic confidence to memorize the dialogue expected of all elders and sisters. I questioned how he could be so successful as a servant of the Lord without being able to learn his discussions even after months in the field. I was fascinated with the idea of an elder who seemingly did not have a grasp on the words he was supposed to teach, but who still had the ability to bring souls to the waters of baptism. In my youthful rationalization, I dismissed him as one who must be cutting corners. I reasoned that there was no right way to do something wrong. How could he be doing things the right way if he didn't even know the discussions? Since I was his zone leader, it would be easy enough for me to find out.

I secured an appointment to work with him for a night. I made sure on that particular evening we would be door contacting. My experience had led me to the belief that nothing reveals the strengths and weaknesses of a missionary more than tracting. As his leader I volunteered to take the first few doors. My competitive zeal got the best of me, and with the intensity of a door-to-door salesman, I placed a Book of Mormon in almost every home. With the pride of a Zoramite standing on the Rameumptom, I turned to Elder Jarvis and said, "Why don't you give it a try?"

With an "ah shucks" kind of shrug, he replied, "I'll do my best."

Before the next door opened, I glanced over at him. The thought came to me, "He looks like he'd be more comfortable baling hay than knocking on doors."

The sun was going down and the street lamp had little effect in shedding light on the porch in which we were standing. From every observable perspective to that point in the evening, it seemed to me that Elder Jarvis was severely lacking in confidence. I had worked with many elders before, but I had never worked with one who was so empty in basic poise. It baffled me that he could have been so successful while lacking what I thought were the bare necessities of missionary work.

Just then, the door opened, and we were greeted by an Englishman about a foot shorter than either one of us. It was apparent by his body language that he was not interested in us or our message at all. I refer to his body language rather than his facial expression because it was too dark to see much of his face.

My companion pierced the silence with the standard door approach. "Hi, my name is Elder Jarvis and this is my mate Elder Ba. . ." He was quickly interrupted by the words, "I'm busy and I'm not really interested."

Surely, my mate knew it was his turn to speak. (*Mate* is a synonym for companion in England). It was amazing how long the empty seconds were stretching the time as we stood in total silence in the semi-darkness waiting for Elder Jarvis to say something—anything. He was trying to speak, but the words just weren't finding their way out. I was surprised that this Englishman had not closed the door and even more surprised that my companion from Arizona seemed to have swallowed his tongue. As I glanced in his direction, he was obviously trying to do his part, but it just wasn't happening. He looked about as tongue-tied as a befuddled teenager on his first date. There we were, the three of us—an uncomfortable Englishman, a missionary frozen in silence, and me.

After the pause, which seemed to be eternal, my mate reached through the darkened doorway and placed what must have felt like a bear claw on the undersized man's shoulder. With his other hand he did something that will never be found in the missionary handbook. In the shadowy twilight, he threw a light-hearted mock punch toward the mid-section of the surprised Englishman. Elder Jarvis must have found his voice because he blurted out, "Ah, c'mon, let us in for a few minutes so we can share what we know is true."

He stood there with a big grin on his face and waited for a reply. I thought, "Oh, my gosh, I'm gonna spend the night in an English jail! How am I going to explain this to my parents."

I could hardly believe what happened next. This man who had been so cold just a few seconds before, stepped back and said, "Well, I suppose I can take a few moments to hear your message."

He was even smiling when he said it!

I was beginning to see Elder Jarvis's magic. At that moment he had such pure love that everything else that he lacked as a missionary didn't seem to matter. He was like a human fountain of charity, which overflowed in the direction of everyone with whom he came in contact. This was my first exposure to a fellow missionary who had no other agenda than loving and accepting everyone. In an instant it was felt and welcomed by this total stranger. I felt it too, and there in a place so far away from my home, I felt at home because of *his* charity.

Our newfound friend ushered us into his home, and we presented the Joseph Smith story. True to his word, he wasn't interested. After some warm conversation and a cool drink of water, he allowed us to leave a blessing on his home. As he graciously escorted us to the door, his parting words were full of encouragement and hope that our time in England would be enjoyable.

As we rode our bikes toward our apartment, the thought came to me that no one in our mission could have gotten through that door except Elder Jarvis. And though I was his leader, he was the one who had been teaching me on that evening. I was convinced that his humility had made him totally unaware of his greatness. Maybe that is true of all people who have genuine spirituality. With no strategy in mind, he melted the hearts of all the people he came in contact with—including mine. He was an object lesson for the pure love of Christ. In comparison to the charity that radiated from Elder Jarvis, my way of dealing with people up to that point blew in the breeze like a paperback copy of *How to Win Friends and Influence People.* Perhaps that is what the Apostle Paul meant when he wrote these words, "Though I speak with the tongue of . . . angels and have not charity, I am, as sounding brass, or a tinkling cymbal" (1 Corinthians 13:1).

Years later I was teaching seminary in Arizona. Totally unaware of the fact that the former Elder Jarvis had married and was living in the area, I had occasion to share this story with the Saints in that community as a columnist for the *Latter-day Sentinel.* His wife read my account of her husband as a missionary. She called me on the phone and invited my wife and me to their home to enjoy a wonderful dinner of fish and chips. She told me during the evening that what I had seen in Elder Jarvis was the thing that first attracted her to him and was still a major part of his personality.

It was as a missionary that I first recognized that "perfect love casteth out all fear" (Moroni 8:16). The scripture doesn't say "some fear," or even "most fear." Without hesitation Moroni states, "all fear." As one who has had the opportunity to stand and deliver the gospel in about as many settings as can be imagined, I can testify that oftentimes my heart has been filled with worry, stress, anxiety, fear of failure, and all the associated maladies that can come under the heading of fear. I have discovered the perfect prescription for this dilemma has been to genuinely love the people I am serving. When I am honestly not concerned with their acceptance of me but am totally absorbed in concern for their welfare, the Spirit makes the best of what I offer.

The best way for me to handle negative stress (in situations ranging from an ornery neighbor to the driver who sees the freeway as his personal race track) is perfect love. You might say, "Well, that's not going to change them." My response is this is not about changing others; it's about changing me. Love doesn't make everyone conform to my wishes, but it directly connects me to the solution rather than the problem. It clears the head as well as the soul and has an amazing effect on the health and well-being of the body.

II. Attack the Man in the Bear Suit.

I know a story that perfectly illustrates the concept of attacking those fears that are creations of our own thinking. A man named Frank met with a therapist because he wanted to reinvent himself socially, but was paralyzed with the thought of asking anyone out on a date. His reasons for this were well-founded due to the fact that his once-happy marriage came to an abrupt end when his wife called it quits.

There was a woman at his work whom he wished to ask out but could not find the courage to do so. The therapist asked him how motivated he was to solve his problem on a scale from one to ten. He was confident that surely he was a ten.

The therapist assured him that while success would not be easy it could be achieved in one day. Her assessment of his problem was due to his fear of rejection. Therefore, she proposed to put him in a setting where he would be exposed to seventy-five rejections in one day. His task was to go to a nearby shopping mall, and while carefully approaching women near a coffee shop, he was to say, "Hi, my name is Frank. I hope you don't think I'm rude, but I'm wondering if you would like to have coffee with me."

After enduring this for awhile, he was to migrate over to an escalator and repeat the same line to women coming off the moving staircase. He was to keep track of the number of rejections, and when the count achieved was seventy-five, his goal would be complete. Obviously, he was advised to use good judgment and to rotate between the various escalators in the large mall so he would not be seen as a threat by the store management. He was to call the therapist when the assignment was completed.

Frank began by quickly obtaining three rejections near the coffee shop. His confidence was growing until a woman accepted his invitation, which made him realize that obtaining seventy-five rejections may take a little longer than he had hoped. He moved to a new location and immediately obtained five more rejections. His confidence was growing once again. His plan hit a roadblock when several women said yes. The loss of time was an irritation. Not to mention the consumption of so much coffee.

He then made a plan that he felt would be sure to work. He would ask women who (in his mind) were obviously out of his league. Even this was not a complete success. His motivation, which began as a ten, had now declined to a two. He then spotted a gorgeous woman approaching the down escalator. She was a least six inches taller than himself and was ultra-fashionable in her silver mini-dress. Her gaze was one that could best be defined as ice-cold. He was confident that his lack of interest in her would be surely reciprocated. This would be such a challenge that he decided to give himself fifteen bonus points.

As she glided down the escalator, Frank recognized the ridiculousness of the situation. The thought came to him that even with the bonus points he would still need thirty more rejections to reach his goal. This idea only served to make him tired.

He thought of the lady at his work whom he thought was attractive. Quickly, he took out his cell phone and dialed her number. Undeterred by her answering machine, he heard himself saying, "Hi, this is Frank. I hope you don't think I'm rude, but I'm wondering if you would like to have coffee with me."

Because of what he had been through that day, he was totally unfazed when she returned his call and politely refused his invitation. Several days later he asked out a woman from the neighborhood who accepted, and as they say, "The rest is history."

Success would have been impossible for Frank had he not accepted that his fear was all in his head. As I referred to earlier in this chapter, he symbolically ripped the head off the bear suit only to discover that he was the man inside. Frank placed himself solely in charge of his symptom as well as his solution. Perhaps this specific solution would not be appropriate for everyone in Frank's situation, but the principle involved is still correct.

Robert Millet wrote,

> The wisest among us . . . refuse to allow fear to set our agenda. One of the leaders of the Church once related to a group of us that not long after he had been called as a General Authority someone planted a bomb at the door of the Salt Lake Temple. The bomb had exploded and knocked the large, heavy door off its hinges. He commented that the episode was chilling to him and created an anxiety and discomfort, a fear, that lasted all day. To his utter surprise, he noticed that all through the day, in the many meetings he attended with other General Authorities, no mention was made of this scary incident. Finally, at the end of the day, he asked one of the senior Brethren about the temple door, only to have his colleague remark, "Yes, we need to get that fixed, don't we?" Then he added this important principle, one that ought to guide our walk and talk as we move into troublesome days ahead: "We do not take counsel from our fears."[1]

This truth has echoed through the ages. Many years earlier in the Civil War "when Stonewall Jackson planned a daring attack, one of his generals fearfully objected, saying, 'I am afraid of this' or 'I fear that . . .' Putting his hand on his timorous subordinate's shoulder, Jackson said, 'General, never take counsel of your fears.' "[2]

Many centuries earlier, Moses was confronted by Satan. The record states, "Moses began to fear exceedingly; and as he began to fear, he saw the bitterness of hell" (Moses 1:20).

What a graphic description of the road we travel when our hearts are filled with fear. Moses did not have to die to get a glimpse of hell. He didn't even have to commit the sins, which would send him to the location known as hell. All Moses had to do to get a taste of the place is to "fear exceedingly," and he "saw the bitterness of hell." What a powerful statement about the road we travel when our hearts are filled with fear. No wonder, as Elder Packer stated, we "frequently seek relief from counseling, from analysis, and even medication."[3]

Without discounting the place of these professionals in our problems, the scripture continues, "Nevertheless, calling upon God, he received strength" (Moses 1:20).

Moses chose the solution stated by the Lord Himself, "Look unto me in every thought; doubt not, fear not" (D&C 6:36).

With the Lord on our side, we not only deal with the men in bear suits, which are the creations of our own imaginations, but, as the story of Moses teaches, we can also deal with those justifiable fears not of our own imaginings.

An account from the life of the Prophet Wilford Woodruff illustrates this truth. On one of his many missionary journeys, Elder Woodruff and his companion approached a grove of trees. A large black bear came out toward them. "We were not afraid of him," he said, "for we were on the Lord's business, . . . When the bear got within eight rods of us [a distance of about 44 yards or 40 meters] he sat on his haunches and looked at us a moment, and then ran away; and we went on our way rejoicing."[4] When we are comfortable in the knowledge that we are on the Lord's errand, it is much easier to leave so many things, including our fears, in the hands of the Lord.

In group settings, I like to do an activity that illustrates the power of our thoughts—the power of our fears. I divide the auditorium into three equally sized groups. I remind them that in order for the experiment to work, I need complete silence. I direct groups two and three to put their heads down and not look up until I tell them to do so. I ask group one (who have their heads up) to silently study the three words I then project on the screen behind me. The words on the screen are *terrified*, *afraid*, and *scared*. I then remove the words while inviting them to put their heads down, and with their eyes closed silently review the words they have just seen.

I then ask group two to lift up their eyes to the screen while I invite groups one and three to keep their heads down. I then place a different set of words on the screen for the second group. The words are *valentine*, *sweetheart*, and *darling*. Now, group two is invited to join group one with their heads down, pondering their three words.

Group three is asked to raise their eyes to the screen where I show the words *yogi*, *smoking*, and *polar*. For the next few moments, all three groups are asked to place their heads down and silently ponder the three words I have given them. Each person present is only aware of the three words I have given their group. With their heads down, I tell them I am placing a four letter word on the screen with one of the letters left out and that in a moment I will ask them to lift their heads up and look at the word. They are to continue to think about the three words even as they are viewing the word on the screen. With no effort at all, their minds will fill in the blank letter to complete the word. I also ask them to continue their silence because I would like to predict what they are thinking.

The word I place on the screen is _EAR. I turn to group one and say, "With no effort on your part beyond pondering the three words, the word on the screen you have seen is FEAR." When I request a show of hands as to the affirmative, almost all hands go up. I then turn to group two and say, "Almost all of you completed the word as DEAR." To which all, or close to it, agree. Turning to group three, I state that their word has become BEAR. Usually, with some chuckles through the crowd, they acknowledge my prediction was correct. It's fascinating how people look at class members in other groups and question how in the world they could come up with fear, dear, or bear. It reminds me how easy it is to judge others when we are convinced that our perspective is correct.

Next, I place all nine words on the screen in this fashion, so they can finally obtain a view of other perspectives:

Group 1	Group 2	Group 3
Terrified	Valentine	Yogi
Afraid	Sweetheart	Smokey
Scared	Darling Polar	

I remind them that we do not see the world as it is; we see the world as we are. Without any stimulus other than three words, I was able predict the thoughts of an auditorium of people. No humor, no drama, no emotion whatsoever—just three words placed in their heads, and to a certain degree, their thoughts were predictable. Our behavior then becomes the sum total of what is in our minds and our hearts. Perhaps a portion of the violent behavior we see escalating in our society is connected to fear. The challenge is in replacing our fears with faith and hope. I will elaborate on this point later in the book.

III. Service

Many years ago I was doing some research using the index in the back of the triple combination. As I looked up the word *leader,* what I found was indeed unexpected. There were no references to the Doctrine and Covenants or the Pearl of Great Price. What surprised me even more was that it was only referenced in the Book of Mormon six times, and out of this, four of the references were negative. (The actual number of times the word *leader* or *leaders* is used in the Book of Mormon is forty-six.) I then moved to the word *servant* in the index and found a fascinating contrast with the word *leader.* The word *servant* was listed nineteen times in the Doctrine and Covenants and four times in the Pearl of Great Price. As I looked under the heading entitled *servant,* I discovered fifteen references in the Book of Mormon. The fascinating contrast comes when we recognize that it is only listed negatively once. (The actual number of times the word *servant* or *servants* is used in the Book of Mormon is 137 times.)

What an amazing contrast; I was fascinated by not only the number of times the word *servant* was used as compared to the word *leader,* but how often the word *leader* was used in a negative sense while the word *servant* is used almost exclusively in the Book of Mormon in a positive vein. I did not then nor do I now see this as happenstance. It is not hard to remember how many times my life has been blessed by a leader who saw himself as a servant.

In November 1973, shortly before my wife and I were married, she went with a group of friends to present a homemade quilt to President Spencer W. Kimball and his wife, Camilla, to mark the occasion of their fifty-sixth wedding anniversary. I was graciously allowed to travel with the group to the home of President and Sister Kimball to deliver the gift.

As we pulled unannounced into the driveway of a modest brick home, the thought occurred to me that this was not a house purchased with the intent of drawing attention to its owner. Within minutes we had emptied the car of its occupants and were standing at the front door. Moments after we rang the bell, the door opened, and in its frame stood the man we had come to honor. Even though we had no appointment and were surely interrupting time to be with his wife, his face lit up, and he said, "My young friends, how can I be of service to you?"

If we didn't impress him with our voices, at least he appeared to appreciate our enthusiasm as we sang a song honoring the occasion. He then did something I had never seen before. Taking one person at a time by the hand, he led us individually to the living room. The process was repeated until all of us had been personally delivered by the Prophet. I thought how much easier it would have been for this elderly man to just bring us in with a wave and a smile. His manner reminded me of the "one by one" approach by the Savior in 3 Nephi 11.

After we had been seated comfortably, he disappeared into the next room for a moment. He returned accompanied by his radiant companion, Camilla. The tender way he introduced his wife was consistent with the behavior we witnessed since our arrival. Like a grandfather, he declared to the group of college students: "I have a refrigerator full of milk and cookies that I would be happy to serve you."

He disappeared into the kitchen only to return to fulfill his desire to serve us snickerdoodles and milk. While this was happening, I was a bit dazed with the thought that we had come uninvited to his home following what I'm sure had been an exhausting work day, and the entire time he had been serving our needs.

One of us finally remembered to present the quilt. I'm sure this gift was only one of many gifts they had received in the past few days, but their gracious manner made us feel like it was just what they needed.

After a short visit, we bade the Prophet and his wife farewell. Once again they considered our needs by following us to the snowy edge of the front porch and encouraged us to have a safe journey. A passerby might have thought that an elderly couple were waving to their grandchildren as we pulled out of the driveway.

We drove in silence for a few blocks as each of us digested our experience of the past twenty minutes. Finally, the moment was interrupted by one of the girls in the backseat. "I don't know what it will feel like to stand in the presence of the Lord someday. But if it's anything like being in the presence of Spencer W. Kimball, I can't wait."

I believe she summed it up for all present. However, as the years have passed, I see the experience with a somewhat different perspective. At the time, I thought we had felt that way was because President Kimball was a great leader. While that is certainly true, I have learned that the greatness of his leadership was because he was a servant to all. The events of that evening were a microcosm of his approach to leadership, life, and service.

You might question what this has to do with dealing with the host of negatives I have placed under the heading of fear. When we are engaged in fear and its accompanying friends, it is easy for our world to get dark, stale, and very self-absorbed. President Kimball spoke to the solution. "When we are engaged in the service of our fellowmen . . . we put our problems in a fresher perspective. When we concern ourselves with others, there is less time to be concerned with ourselves! In the midst of the miracle of serving, there is the promise of Jesus that by losing ourselves, we find ourselves!"[5]

This process of finding ourselves really becomes the search in choosing our best self. For example, many years ago, I was visiting with one of my female students who was struggling with her spiritual identity. In the midst of our conversation, she interrupted with words that gasped from the depths of her soul, "I would know who I was if there was not so many of me!"

She had more in common with the rest of us than she understood. We are all capable of wearing many personalities. It is our responsibility to choose our best self and stay the course. President Kimball's words would indicate that this choosing is made much easier while we lose ourselves in the service of others.

His life seemed to reflect this approach. In 1985 President Kimball was to lead a group of brethren through a series of area conferences in New Zealand and Australia. However, he was left behind in Salt Lake City to have emergency surgery. President N. Eldon Tanner lead the group in his place. President Tanner called the Prophet's hospital room each day to get a report on his condition and to give a report on the conferences. Elder H.

Burke Peterson related the following regarding one of those days: "President Tanner made his usual call to the hospital. . . . When we asked if he had talked to the President, he told us he had tried, but President Kimball wasn't in his room. 'Where was he?' we asked. 'They weren't sure; they couldn't find him,' President Tanner said. 'They thought he might have gone down to the next floor of the hospital to visit the sick.' "[6] President Kimball had every reason to be self-absorbed in his own ill health, but he chose his best self through service.

President Gordon B. Hinckley spoke about this "self choosing": "Generally speaking, the most miserable people I know are those who are obsessed with themselves. . . . The most effective medicine . . . is to lose ourselves in the service of others. . . . The best challenge for weariness is the challenge of helping someone who is even more tired."[7]

It is hard to imagine that this great Prophet contemplated coming home early from his mission as a young man in England due to discouragement. The words of his father, quick and to the point, serve as a reminder to all of us. "Forget yourself and go to work."[8]

It is in this "forgetting" and serving that we truly find ourselves.

Over the past eleven years, I have had the exhilarating experience on numerous occasions to ride as a patient in an ambulance to the emergency rooms of various hospitals, as well as to their intensive care units. In fact, based on the gowns that are (almost) worn in the intensive care units, I have come to the conclusion that ICU really stands for "I See You." I finally figured out why mooning isn't nearly as appreciated while wearing a hospital gown. Totally lost in the process is the element of surprise. The three heart attacks I have experienced in a little over a decade have placed me on a first name basis with our health care professionals. I fear that if this habit keeps up, I may get a plaque on the wall of a Utah Valley hospital.

Crises like these have been a great teacher to me when I have let them. The fear, pain, and emotional instability as a patient are normal. However, I have discovered that it is possible to rise above my problems by genuinely getting beyond myself in the service of others. In fact, this very book is the result of my third heart attack and the need to get beyond myself. I began writing this book within days after returning from the hospital. In times like these, I have painfully discovered that pity parties have come too easily for me. The hardest time for me to be a servant is when it seems to me that I deserve every one waiting on me.

When I had my latest heart attack, my most enjoyable moments in the hospital were the times in the intensive care unit when I took my walks through the halls. I tried to stop at each room to offer encouragement to the other patients. As I passed by the doctors and nurses, I attempted to say something funny or at least cheery and uplifting. In truth my heart was crying out, and I wanted to stop everyone in listening range and discuss what a bad break I had received and pass out invitations to my pity party. But by forgoing the negative and serving others instead, I have found it easier to heal. It has been my experience that physical healing is aided immeasurably by ridding myself of all those elements under the heading of fear. I know too well that this approach goes against elements of modern psychology—the Gospel often does.

Six years ago after my second heart attack, I returned home in a rough state. My heart had obviously been through a trauma, but it seemed that I was mentally and emotionally in the darkest abyss. Apparently, I had remained under anesthesia for an extended period of time in surgery and the effect on my emotional and mental chemistry really set me back. For days I sat around sinking further and further into a hole, and I seemed powerless to pull myself out of it. The medications and drugs I received for the problem offered me little solution. Finally, I pulled out the directory for the little community of Mona, Utah in which I lived. I identified two people in town who, in my opinion, were worse off than myself. For the next few months I went to their houses to bring them books, videos, food, and light conversation. I was conscious at all times to stay away from pity parties. We poked fun and laughed at our conditions but rarely stayed long in any conversation which might be considered negative. I just couldn't go there, and I believed it wasn't in their best interest either. I became such good friends with these people by becoming part of their solution rather than their problem. By forgetting myself and choosing my better self through service, the mental and emotional clouds that hung over me were blown away over time.

IV. As If

Many years ago as a young missionary in England I was introduced to this principle which has had a profound effect on my life. I supposed it could be best stated, "Act the part until the part becomes you." We are constantly involved in this process, but rarely as a conscious venture. It is closely related to this choosing of our best selves I mentioned in section

III. My mission president was Wallace Bennett, a man I hold second only to my own father. He introduced me to so many wonderful things just by being the man he was. One of his friends was a member of the Seventy named Sterling W. Sill, who had written a few books that President Bennett introduced to me. I digested them like a starving man at a Thanksgiving feast. I was confronted by the "As If" principle through two of these books. Rather than dissect the principle, I will just share two stories from Elder Sill:

> A recent news release told of the "Passion Play" given every ten years in the little Bavarian village of Oberammergau wherein a group of players re-enact the last week in the life of Christ. The play has been put on regularly since the year 1633. Each player accepts the part he is to play, and then he lives that part and nothing else, until that is what he becomes. The one who plays the part of Jesus must think like Jesus and act like Jesus and feel like Jesus. Can you imagine what the result would be in his life? Or can you imagine the possible power of this "as if" principle in our individual lives if we would just select the role in life that we wished to play and then live the part twenty-four hours per day?
>
> This particular news report of the "Passion Play" gave an interesting item about a man who recently committed suicide. For the previous five years he had been taking the part of Judas. But that is not all. This was the third Judas in recent years who had come to his death by suicide. If he had lived like Judas and thought like Judas, what is more natural than that he should have died like Judas? . . .
>
> Pick out any part in life that you wish to play and then play it with all your heart, and that is what you will become. It is as simple as that. . . .
>
> The only inferiority that is in us is what we ourselves put there. . . . You get the role in life which you yourself select."[9]

The second story by Elder Sill has resonated in me for thirty-six years.

> Bunker Bean's parents died when he was but a child, and he was left alone in the world. He "roamed the earth in rags and timidly through its terrors." Because he was inferior many of his friends made fun of him. And his mind was full of fears. He was afraid of policemen; he was afraid to ride in the elevator, as each time the elevator seemed to fall he suffered the sensations of dying. He was afraid of the future, afraid of situations, afraid of things, afraid of life—afraid of himself.

Then one day a false spiritualistic medium moved into the cheap boarding-house where Bunker Bean lived. This man had a book on reincarnation, and he persuaded young Bunker Bean to believe that as we cast off our worn-out shoes and replace them with new, so we cast off our worn-out bodies and reclothe our spirits by this process of reincarnation.

Bunker Bean believed wholeheartedly in the teaching of his new-found friend. . . . This man persuaded Bunker Bean that in return for his savings and a part of his wages over a long period, he could tell him Bunker Bean's previous incarnations. . . .

Bunker Bean was surprised and delighted to learn the he, the weak, timid Bunker Bean, had once been the great Napoleon Bonaparte, the master of the world. It was quite a shock to learn that once people had been afraid of him. When he had been Napoleon the world had trembled before him. Then policemen had been to him as insects.

This he could not understand, and so he inquired of his friend why it was that Napoleon had been so courageous and Bunker Bean so timid. The medium explained that life went in vast karmic cycles. Napoleon had lived on the upper half of the cycle when the qualities of courage, initiative and power had been in the ascendancy. But Bunker Bean lived in the lower part of the cycle that was characterized by timidity, fear and weakness. Therefore, Bunker Bean possessed the exact opposites of the great Napoleonic courage and self-confidence. . . .

He was told by his friend that the lower part of the cycle was just now being completed and he was re-entered that period in which he had lived so famously as Napoleon the Great. . . . He would soon feel a strange life stirring within him, for he was even now well on the way to becoming his own inspired, courageous, determined self again—strong, self-reliant, fearless and successful.

Even the thought of who he really was made Bunker Bean expand his chest. He straightened his shoulders and studied himself in the glass. Now that he thought about it, there was a certain majesty in his look. The thought of who he was and of his former accomplishments made him vibrate with a strange, fresh power never known before. He went to the library, where he secured and enthusiastically read every book about Napoleon, his former self. . . .

He collected pictures of Napoleon and hung them around his little attic room where he could feast his mind upon them. He imitated the speech, thoughts and acts of his former self. . . .

He thought, "What would Napoleon have done?" And he knew that Napoleon would have been contemptuous of the groundless fears which had so terrorized the early life of Bunker Bean.

One of the historians had said that Napoleon had "won his battles in his tent." That was good enough for Bunker Bean. He would also plan and organize and think the problem out before it came to trial, just as Napoleon had done. Like Napoleon he would see to it that nothing was left to chance. Napoleon had permitted no exceptions to success. Bunker Bean had a colored picture of Napoleon sitting on his great white [horse] . . . overlooking a crucial battle. . . .

Napoleon had exhibited his greatest powers as he led men to conquest. Inasmuch as there were now no wars to be fought, Bunker Bean must find some other outlet for his extraordinary abilities. He had been employed in a minor position in a business undertaking. . . . Bunker Bean knew that what he had once accomplished on the field of battle he would now repeat in the field of commerce. . . . He felt sure that if he followed the principles that had been so productive in the past, he could not fail in the future.

The historians had said that Napoleon "had known human nature like a book." Therefore, he resolved to study human nature. The historian had said that "with Napoleon, to think was to act," also that Napoleon was "merciless in driving himself." Therefore Bunker Bean would do again all of these things which had previously laid the world at his feet. . . .

He was soon a different person. And other people began to notice the changes that were taking place in him. As a consequence, he was given more important work assignments, his pay was increased, and he began to advance with great rapidity up the positive incline of his success cycle. Now he knew that his friend had told him the truth.

Then he was struck with another thought. He knew that for a short period of 52 years, he had been Napoleon. But certainly he should have some information about himself over a longer period. Who was he before he had been Napoleon? With these questions he again confronted his friend, and now that prosperity and money were coming his way, he could pay the medium well for whatever additional information could be obtained.

After the money had been paid, he learned to his further astonishment and delight that before he had been Napoleon he had been the greatest of the Egyptian Pharaohs. He had had a long and wonderful reign and had died at the age of 82 years. His death was deeply mourned by all of his people. He, Rameses, had been a ruler of great strength and character. . . .

As the Pharaoh, he had been tall and handsome. He was so impressed with the account of the magnificence of the physical bearing of the Pharaoh that he immediately employed the best tailor and had his clothing cut in such a way as to give him the appearance of perfect physical development. The effect produced so improved his form that he unconsciously strove to develop the appearance that the garment gave him. He expanded his chest, drew in his waist and stood erect. . . .

He understood that such a marked advance in his spirit could not all be made in a day. Such progress could only come after long dwelling in thought and practice upon the qualities that were responsible for his splendid past. . . .

No longer would he play the coward before trivial adversaries. He would direct large affairs; he would think big. . . . Never again would he be afraid of death, or life, or policemen, or the mockery of his fellows. Under this mental discipline his spirit grew tall and its fibers toughened. . . .

Strength seemed to flow into him from his mental image of the strong, calm demeanor of the Pharaoh. . . . He had once ruled a mighty people in Egypt. But also centuries later he had been Napoleon and had made Europe tremble under the tread of his victorious armies. . . . Bunker Bean believed himself to be both a wise king and a courageous soldier. He thought courage at night and he awoke in the morning with a giant's strength. His thoughts . . . gave him an iron will.

Then one day Bunker Bean made a tragic discovery. The medium was a fake. None of these important things that he had believed were true. He had been cheated for the sake of his money. Then he realized the he was not a king, that he was only weak, timid Bunker Bean, mean and insignificant. What a tremendous let-down! What an occasion for dejection and discouragement!

But in the years that Bunker Bean had believed himself a king, he had formed the habits that go with success, and habits are not easily broken. It was now natural for him to do the things that great men did. . . .

When he had believed himself to be a king, he had been a king. When he had believed himself weak, he had been weak. Had he not discovered the deception and gone on believing in himself, all would have been as before. Then he learned the great truth, that "believing is all that matters.". . .

> During these years no one had known that he had believed himself to be Rameses and Napoleon had been only a crude bit of scaffolding on which he had climbed to success.
>
> But the confidence that he had developed in himself could not endure without the help of the scaffolding. . . . In spite of the discovery, his faith would still continue. . . .
>
> Emotion surged into the eyes of Bunker Bean, threatening to overwhelm him as he contemplated these great truths that "every man is born a king," "Every man is born to riches." "To believe is all that matters.' "[10]

It would be a short journey in each person's life to find examples of the As If principle, both positive and negative. I mentioned at the beginning of the book how insecure I felt as a young teenager with myself physically and how the words that I digested from one so admired regarding my ability to high jump had such a profound affect on me. Another thing which bothered me throughout my youth was that I was terribly pigeon toed. This is when the feet point inward when a person walks or even stands. It was easy for me to trip on stairs, or stumble as I stepped off the curb unless I was paying attention. When I was a small child, my mother took me to a doctor who suggested that either I could have surgery to correct the problem or I could walk to school each day like a duck with my toes pointing to the outside. So for the next few years, I would purposely place my heel on the line in the middle of the sidewalk that stretched straight ahead of me. In so doing, my feet were pointed to the outside rather than my natural pigeon-toed approach to walking. At those times I put the words of the doctor into practice, and I truly walked like a duck.

However, when I was running or not paying attention, I was just me. It was not unusual to have people periodically point out (sometimes in insensitive manner) that my approach to foot travel was not normal. It wasn't that big of a deal, but it was always there—annoying and kind of like pimples to a teenager on prom night.

Then, one Sunday in sacrament meeting in the Yuba City Second Ward, we had a guest speaker. Through the years I have forgotten if he was a former athlete from the area or a coach. But he was someone who had my attention, as well as my respect. I was sitting on the stand as the bishop's messenger, which usually required nothing more than sitting on the stand. But in the middle of the guest speaker's talk, the bishop leaned over to me and asked me to do something that necessitated me to leave the chapel.

Dutifully, I walked past the pulpit, down the aisle, and into the foyer area. All the while listening intently to what was coming from the pulpit.

Just as I stepped from view of the chapel, the speaker stopped his talk. I halted in my tracks, wondering what was wrong. The silence was interrupted with these words, "Who was that kid who just walked out of this room?"

Like a tattle-tale someone from the congregation announced my name. He continued, "Did you see the way he was walking, with his toes pointed inward."

Embarrassed and ashamed, my heart leaped into my throat. I felt naked before the ward. Fighting back my tears, I wanted to run from that building and never come back. I just knew what was coming could not be good. Then, came the transforming power of what I have since understood to be the As If principle.

As a young teenager his words echoed in my heart like a present from heaven, which has been with me till this day. I will remember his words forever, "The way he walks is a gift from God. Only the finest sprinters have that gift. That boy is an athlete." Then he went on to give a short treatise regarding the advantage it is to have your feet turned in when you run.

I disappeared into the restroom as emotion filled to overflowing. I went into a stall, leaned against the wall, and wept out the last few years of frustration and social embarrassment. Those words from someone I respected with all my heart were digested in such a way, beginning with that day, my shame was replaced with a calmness that has made me totally unaware of anyone else's opinion regarding the way I walk.

At this point in my life, I'm not so sure how much of what he said is technically true, and it doesn't really matter. But at that age, to that boy, coming from that man, I was elevated to new heights of self-confidence. As I walked naturally with confidence, I became totally disconnected to the eyes and opinions of those around me regarding what had formally been considered a disability. In fact, on those occasions that it was mentioned, I took it either as a compliment or as ignorance on their part that they just didn't recognize an athlete when they saw one. From disability to ability—not because of what he had said, but because of what I believed. Everyone else in the congregation heard what he said, but I'm confident that no one else digested his words down to their soul.

Such is the power of the As If principle: Act the part until the part becomes you! Can we not see the transforming power of the scriptures in this principle. Slowly, over time we begin to digest the scriptures on a daily basis. Our thoughts are elevated continually to a higher spiritual plain. Then, as we continue over an extended period, the scriptures begin to digest us in the sense that our thoughts as well as our behavior have improved. If Bunker Bean's life changed when he began to study Napoleon and Rameses (even though his study was based on a false premise), think of the power of the As If principle in our lives as we study the Savior and the words of the prophets.

Notes

1. Robert Millet, *I Will Fear No Evil: How the Lord Sustains Us in Perilous Time* (Salt Lake City: Bookcraft, 2002), 18.
2. Norman Vincent Peale, *The Power of Positive Thinking*, 24.
3. Boyd K. Packer, in Conference Report, Apr. 1978, 139–40.
4. *Teachings of Presidents of the Church—Wilford Woodruff* (The Church of Jesus Christ of Latter-day Saints: Salt Lake City, 2004), 153.
5. Spencer W. Kimball, "The Abundant Life," *Ensign*, Jul. 1978, 3–7.
6. H. Burke Peterson, in Conference Report, Apr. 1985, 81–82.
7. Gordon B. Hinckley, *Standing for Something* (New York: Times Books, 2000), 56.
8. See Jeffrey R. Holland, "President Gordon B. Hinckley: Stalwart and Brave He Stands," *Ensign*, Jun. 1995, 8.
9. Sterling W. Sill, *Leadership* (Salt Lake City: Bookcraft, 1960), 31–34.
10. Sterling W. Sill, *The Power of Believing* (Salt Lake City: Bookcraft, 1968), 17–25.

chapter three

Anger and the Unforgiving Heart

A FEW YEARS AGO, I HAD AN OLD Geo Metro that saved me a lot on gas during the eighty-four miles I traveled to and from work each day. Typical of elderly vehicles, it had some unique special features. One that I always had to be mindful of was that it had a very strong inclination to digest oil. It was so consistent in its appetite that after a while I didn't even need to check the dip stick to see if it needed oil. Based on experience, I knew that at the end of a two week period, I would need to put in another quart of oil. I tried to take care of such matters in the evening so that I wouldn't have to hustle around in the morning and make myself late to work.

One night, I asked my teenage son Blaine to put a quart of oil in the vehicle, which he dutifully carried out. The next morning progressed like any other day until I traveled on the freeway about half the distance to work. I begin to smell something I assumed was diesel fuel coming from one of the trucks just ahead of me. The smell continued even after I exited the freeway. That's when I began to suspect that the stench must be coming from a source a little bit closer to me.

When I pulled into the underground parking at the institute building, there was absolutely no doubt regarding the source of the problem. When I slowed down, I noticed that the smell was accompanied by a slight puff of smoke. After slipping into my parking space, I lifted up the hood of the car. This slight puff of smoke became a cloud that rose above the engine enough for me to diagnose the problem. There was a cloth rag stuck in the hole where the oil cap went.

In an effort to piece the evidence together, I could see my son losing the oil cap in the dark after he had done what I asked him to do. In his haste he must have stuffed the rag into the hole thinking that eventually the oil cap would be found and returned to its rightful place. In the mean time I was driving a potential "bomb on wheels" to work.

All day long I stewed in my frustration. In my position, a reasonable man would have called up an auto supply shop and found the right oil cap, picked it up on the way home, and later in the evening encouraged his son to let him know about problems like this at the time they occurred—not a day later. Perhaps a reasonable man would extend a slight lecture regarding the dangers of placing someone in such a situation—driving down the freeway in a vehicle that has an oily cloth rag lying on a hot engine.

But my frustration clouded my judgment like the puff of smoke that exited the car when I opened the hood. I made the decision to leave things just as they were and drive the vehicle all the way home so that my son could see the result of his stuffing a rag in the hole that should have housed the oil cap. After all, I reasoned, he would learn best by becoming an eyewitness to the consequences of his actions.

So at the end of the day, I dutifully drove the Metro home. The fact that I was now the one who had placed myself as well as other drivers in harm's way, never crossed my mind. I was firmly entrenched in my role of the "referee" father. With my thoughts racing faster than the Geo Metro, it became completely clear in my clouded mind why my son had done such a foolish thing. Instead of telling me of the mistake when it happened, he had stuffed the rag in the hole hoping he could find the cap and replace it before I discovered the error. With a firm grasp on the obvious, I would return home with all the evidence in place.

The car bravely fought its way home despite losing oil like a soldier giving his last ounce of blood on his final day of battle. By the time the little car limped into the driveway, I wasn't just ready to have a talk with my son—I was psyched!

When I found him out by the barn, I unloaded a full day's worth of frustration on him. At the end of my overblown lecture, I inquired, "Son, why didn't you tell me you had lost the oil cap in the first place?"

To which he replied, "Because I thought you would act the way you're acting right now." I pondered his words for a moment and then asked for a time-out to regroup my emotions for a more suitable presentation.

While his motive for hiding the truth did not excuse his behavior or allow him to avoid the consequences, there was a lesson in this experience for me as well. My frustrations left unchecked escalated into anger that had clouded my judgment. The end result was that by choosing not to get an oil cap and put oil in the car before I returned home, the engine overheated and died shortly thereafter. By playing the role of the radical referee, I became part of the problem rather than the solution.

The Lord admonished the Prophet Joseph to state the truth "not in haste, neither in wrath nor with strife" (D&C 60:14). He also taught, "He that hath the spirit of contention is not of me, but is of the devil" (3 Nephi 11:29). So even if the words I had said to my son were correct, they were "of the devil" because they were delivered in the "spirit of contention." Children and even adults, have a tendency to respond to the method rather than the message when disciplined—such was the case on the occasion of the lost oil cap.

The challenge of introducing anger into the problem can have the same out of control effect as turning a campfire into a forest fire. The prophet Nephi saw that many would wrestle with this challenge in the last days. He observed that those who struggle with anger "belong to [the kingdom of the devil] . . . [and] must be stirred up unto repentance, or the devil will grasp them with his everlasting chains, and they be stirred up to *anger*, and perish" (2 Nephi 28:19, italics added). Notice, how closely "anger" and "perish" are connected.

As one who has dealt with genetic heart disease for over a decade, I can bare personal testimony of the consequences of negative emotions mentioned in chapter one on my health—especially the devastating effects of anger. Anger saps the body of vitality with a poison that seems to be brewed in the bowels of hell.

The idea of "perishing in anger" is echoed by Ammon when he spoke these words to King Lamoni's unrepentant father: "If thou shouldst fall at this time, in thine *anger,* thy soul could not be saved" (Alma 20:17). What a remarkable sentence sermon regarding the danger of anger to the soul possessed by it.

Nephi further observed something, which seems to read like today's newspaper, regarding the younger generation: "At that day shall he rage in the hearts of the children of men, and stir them up to *anger* against that which is good" (2 Nephi 28:20, italics added). I wonder how much of that youthful anger has come as a response to parents who presented (as I did in the oil cap story) the message of truth in an atmosphere of anger.

I had one student say to me that he hated to hear his father tell him he loved him. When I asked him why, he responded, "Because he always tells me he loves me after he chews me out."

Innocent Allies

I believe that conquering anger becomes manageable when we recognize that anger is the result of something that lies beneath the surface of our normal thoughts and behavior. Anger is not necessarily raising one's voice. Anger is often found as an emotional manifestation connected to a spiritual problem that runs much deeper than voice volume. I will define this problem carefully over the next few pages. Let me share a story that happened long ago when I was a seminary teacher for the Church.

Just before a new school year was to start, a female student came into my office to introduce herself. At first she was very enthusiastic, obviously trying to make a positive impression. Her appearance was most appealing, and my initial thought was that she was happy and well adjusted, with a bright outlook on life.

However, as the time passed, I began to notice an attitude that illustrated she had some kind of chip on her shoulder, a type of negativity that didn't seem to be directed toward anyone or anything in particular. It was just a kind of invisible cloud that seemed to hang over her, directing her outlook and thought processes. As she spent more time around me, her everyday behavior began to come through, and it became obvious that something was not right.

I didn't think too much about it until I met her brother, whose enthusiasm and appearance also made for a good first impression. Over time, however, the same negative outlook on life began to surface, especially when the two of them were together. They seemed to be feeding off each other—reinforcing their negativity. They were obviously "at home" when they were jointly criticizing or negatively dissecting something or someone.

I did not choose to confront or openly question their behavior at this time because it had not yet affected those around them in the classroom. I could not discern why they were so dark in their perspective. Their physical health was good, they were not living in poverty, they were not persecuted by their peers, their grades were solid, and their faith did not appear to be in crisis. There were no immediate clues I could see that might reinforce the attitude that encompassed them; then, I met their father.

Once again, the same pattern began to surface: the positive physical appearance, supported by the cheerful and outgoing first impression. Then, over a period of time, as he became more comfortable with me, the chip on his shoulder began to reveal itself. I began to wonder what could be at the root of such a self-destructive attitude.

As the school year progressed, I had a few occasions to visit with their father about various seminary activities, and our paths crossed periodically in the normal comings and goings of everyday life. On one occasion we happened to be visiting in my office, and the conversation turned to more serious matters. He shared with me an experience that helped me understand the negativity I had discerned in him, as well as in his son and daughter.

He related that many years ago, before these two children were born, he had a son who had been the love of his life. Just mentioning the boy brought his emotions to the surface. When the child was but a few years of age, he was joyfully playing in the front yard of their rural home. A drunk driver had misdirected his vehicle through the front fence at a high rate of speed, violently striking the boy. The car continued forward until it slammed against the house.

This good man ran frantically to the aid of his son. Recognizing that the child was in critical need of medical attention, he jumped into his car. He laid his unconscious child across the front seat with the lad's head resting on his lap. As he sped to the nearest hospital, the intoxicated driver of the vehicle that had hit his boy rested comfortably—passed out—still behind the wheel, totally unaware of the deed he had just committed.

My friend arrived at the emergency room within minutes. Clutching his wounded son, he ran through the entrance of the hospital. The waiting room was filled with people due to a serious accident that had just occurred on the freeway. The patients were stranded (some in great distress) because of the minimal numbers of professionals in this small-town emergency room. In this chaos my friend stood holding his wounded son, while the doctors and nurses worked as fast as they could.

Frantically, my friend tried to obtain the necessary attention his son needed right away. It did not take him long to decide that the needs of his son were greater than the number of doctors and nurses available. Instinctively, without full consideration of the consequences, he ran to his car, holding fast to his injured son.

He quickly decided that by driving to another hospital on the other side of town, his son might receive the attention he so desperately needed. At this point, he had no way of knowing how seriously injured the boy really was. Even though his son had not been conscious since the accident and could give no feedback, he felt it was a chance he had to take. As he raced against time, he continually glanced down at his son. Bruised and possibly broken, he appeared to be sleeping. He had no way of knowing what was really happening inside his son's body.

The hospital he was racing toward sat on a small hill. As he approached from a distance his hopes soared. He had taken a chance and everything seemed to be working. Then he noticed the railroad tracks as he approached the base of the hill; as tragic luck would have it, a long train was passing by. Frantically he reasoned, "How could this be? I've never seen a train on these tracks!"

The minutes passed as he sat helpless, his heart beating like never before. He glanced down to see his son had stopped breathing—he was dead!

The telling of his story had ended, but what happened next told another story which bore testimony to the negativity I had witnessed in his children. As I looked into his face I could see a transformation. The tears of mourning for his son were replaced with another kind of emotion. Physically, it was just a continuation of the same tears he had been crying, but emotionally and spiritually he began to cry in a different manner. The change in his face began ever so slightly until it engulfed his whole facial expression. His face became hardened; the pain of loss was replaced with the agony of anger and bitterness, almost revenge.

He looked at me and said, "I hate that drunk driver." He continued, "I hate the doctors and nurses in the emergency room." Then he bowed his head and lamented, "I even hate the conductor of the train."

It is ironic that more than one person on that hate list never even knew of their role in his life on that fateful day. Elder Marion D. Hanks said that forgiving others can "relieve the one aggrieved of the destructive burden that resentment and anger can lay upon us."[1]

It was apparent that this father had found little *relief* regarding his son's passing. He was definitely engulfed in "the destructive burden that resentment and anger can cause."

This good man felt that by directing his anger toward these people, he could be relieved of his terrible burden. He seemed blind to the fact that his pain, as well as his anger, could be completely relieved only by forgiveness.

What a simple remedy to define, and so terribly difficult for this brother, as well as the rest of us, to master. With his sharing of this tragic story, I easily saw that the root of his and his children's expression of anger was the inability to forgive. I believe it is true for many of us.

If only he could have found the strength to do as Nephi did with his brothers Laman and Lemuel following their attempt to take his life: "I did frankly forgive them all that they had done" (1 Nephi 7:21). Think of the wasted energy Nephi would have expended if he had spent himself by seeking revenge against his brothers. His promised land certainly would not have been nearly as "promising." The wasted time and effort, as well as the erosion of peace Nephi spared himself, had taken a terrible toll on my friend. Nephi used his adversity to become *better*, while my friend used his opportunity to become *bitter*. I believe it is in moments such as these that a character is defined, as well as revealed.

Now I was in a better position to understand the chip this man's teenage children carried on their shoulders. It reminded me of the painting by the famous western artist Charles M. Russell, *The Innocent Allies*. The title refers to the horses in the painting that stand dutifully nearby a stagecoach their riders are robbing.

In their formative years these children had stood by as "innocent allies," witnessing the hatred of their father's unforgiving heart. Their father's angry attitude had become a part of them, and as time has carried them well into their adult years, they now have the opportunity to rob their own stagecoaches. As they have matured, hopefully they have learned to use their own agency in choosing a better way. As with all adults, there has come a point in which they can no longer be "innocent allies" but must take responsibility for their own attitudes.

As I mentioned earlier in this chapter, I believe that anger is symptomatic of something deeper. I stated that anger is a emotional manifestation of a spiritual problem. This problem is the "unforgiving heart," the inability to forgive.

The Greater Sin

Anger, hatred, and revenge that come from negatively nurturing an unforgiving heart can turn into something we might never suspect. The Doctrine and Covenants states, "For he that forgiveth not his brother his trespasses standeth condemned before the Lord; for there remaineth in him the greater sin" (D&C 64:9). When I first read this scripture, I wondered how this could be possible. I just couldn't understand how the greater sin could lie with the victim! How is it possible that the greater sin would rest with one such as this good brother and not the drunk driver, simply through his choosing not to forgive?

As my friend related his tragic experience, I began to see how the greater sin could lie with the victim. He had identified the parties responsible for his son's death with the resolve that he could not, and would not, forgive them. What he had not understood is that an unforgiving heart, like its companions anger, hatred, and revenge, is not a laser beam to be directed solely toward those who offend us. These companions are like a double-edged sword that, while they will never fully repay the person who has offended, always sinks its blade deep into the heart of the one holding the weapon.

The proof of this was in this man's hatred of the employees in the emergency room and the conductor of the train—they would probably never be aware of this father's enmity toward them. The sword of the unforgiving heart cut him to the soul without even making contact with those for whom he had ill will.

He had not only become blinded by the damage he had inflicted on himself but was also totally unaware of what he had done to those for which he had no ill will—his own children. He had planted the seed from his unforgiving, and in just a few years, it had grown into a family tree that had unwittingly tied him to his innocent children. They had grown up in close proximity to their father's temperament, and in that environment they had learned to love their friends and hate their enemies. The fruits of this negative family tree are identified as the greater sin.

Like "innocent allies," these children had initially been cut by the sword of hatred just by their mere proximity to their dad, even though his unresolved feelings regarding his son's accident were never consciously directed toward them. These cuts were the emotional scars I had initially sensed in his son and daughter, sending the unmistakable message to everyone to keep their distance. When they spoke negatively about the events and people around them, it was their voices I heard, but the echoing stamp of approval came from their father's example.

By not forgiving, the greater sin becomes a cancer that spreads from one generation to another until its effects are more damaging than the initial transgression. It's not hard to calculate that the sum total of the unforgiving hearts between this father and his children could be more damaging than what the drunk driver had done to his son. What I had seen in these two teens was their father's anger carried on to the next generation—and when would it end? Which generation would have the will to terminate such a negative tradition? Therein would lie the greater sin, spreading like a weed and choking out the promise of charity, service, faith, and the joys of living. These virtues never receive a full chance to grow when they become overtaken by the weeds of anger, hatred, and revenge rooted in an unforgiving heart. This greater sin may take multiple generations to display itself, but for certain, the fallout from one individual's unforgiving heart can create the greater sin over a period of years.

Perhaps this is one of the reasons that Lehi blessed his grandchildren (who were the children of Laman and Lemuel) that their sins would "be answered upon the heads of [their] parents" (2 Nephi 4:6). Though Laman and Lemuel had not been sinned against, they still had unforgiving hearts, and their angry attitude extended through many generations.

Another reason there is a greater sin in the unforgiving heart is that it actively works against the repentance process. If, for example, the drunk driver in the story had any desire to repent, it could have been facilitated by the forgiving heart of a grieving father. An unforgiving heart, however, becomes hardened and unwilling to let the light of repentance seep in anywhere.

The final explanation for the "greater sin" comes in the role of the person who has been sinned against. By not forgiving those who have hurt us, we become judges, taking on the role of Christ and condemning our enemies before their actual day of judgment. Along this line of reasoning, Neal A. Maxwell said that refusing to forgive others is "to hold hostage" those whom the Lord would wish to set free.[2]

Just as the bright virtues of optimism and gratitude are connected, it is also true for the dark companions of anger and the unforgiving heart. Anger is so closely related to the unforgiving heart that it may be difficult to see one without seeing the other. And when the two become welded together, the "greater sin" may be seen in a few generations down the road—waiting to seep its poison into the family tree. I believe this was the road my friend was unknowingly traveling. By not giving all the emotional baggage associated with the tragedy of his son's passing to Christ, my friend was then obligated to carry it himself. What I had witnessed with his children was the inheritance of that baggage unconsciously willed to the next generation. He was a good man, and to see him suffer from this spiritual cancer was painful to witness.

It may be well to add one more element regarding this subject. The greater sin can also be set in motion by not forgiving ourselves. Jeffrey Holland counseled the students of BYU: "We are guilty of the greater sin if we keep remembering and recalling and rebashing someone with their earlier mistakes, and that 'someone' might be ourselves."[3]

Living Life in the Rearview Mirror

Earlier in this book I spent a good deal of time laying out the ramifications of our attitudes on our health. Those with an unforgiving heart digest a poisonous outlook that often becomes too much for their bodies to bear. Many in the medical profession are finally realizing that "ill will" is a major contributor to ill health. I believe that most people don't understand the connection between their physical health and the spiritual doctrine of forgiveness and letting go of the past. In truth, we forgive for our own sake—to help free ourselves of the past and to move forward without baggage.

In my rural community located close to the mountains, my family and I spend time riding four wheelers as well as motorcycles. There is a certain style of motorcycle that can legally be ridden on paved roads as well as "off road." This model of bike is called an Enduro and it has a feature that is not found in the normal "off road" motorcycle: a rearview mirror.

This mirror extends upward from the handlebar no more than one foot, and it leans to the outside. It extends as wide as it safely can, so the rider is able to see what is happening behind him. For the sake of illustration, let's say that you and I are going to attack the face of Mount Nebo, which is located east of my home. We decide that we are going to head up the trail as fast as safely possible. After a few minutes we find ourselves in a comfortable but exhilarating pace that makes the traveling fun.

As we come around a bend in the trail, you (and your Enduro) go down. I swing back just in time to help you off the ground. At first it is unclear if you have hurt anything except your pride. Upon further inspection, we conclude that other than a painful bump on your knee and elbow, you are ready to ride. I then ask why you fell.

Embarrassed that your lack of experience has been revealed, you state that (in your haste) you caught the rearview mirror on a tree limb extending out over the trail. Showing a lack of sensitivity, I say something that could only be funny to someone who had not hurt just his knee, elbow, and pride.

Hopping onto our motorcycles, we resume what began as a joyful journey. However, something within you has changed. You just can't stop thinking about that limb. It was the cause of your injury and embarrassment, and you are unable to let it go. The more you think about it, the madder you get, to the point that (in your anger) you adjust your rear view mirror to get a better look at that "stupid" limb. The more you focus on the limb, the more human it becomes. Even you become convinced that it can make choices—like the choice of knocking you down. You conclude that the limb surely did it on purpose. What had been a small portion of nature's beauty has now turned into a predator, and you have become the victim.

As you adjust your rear view mirror to better focus on the enemy, you conclude, "I'm going to keep my eyes on you so that I will never get hurt like that again."

It doesn't take a prophet to predict what the future will be as you move quickly up the mountain with your eyes firmly fixed in the rearview mirror—the immediate future will be filled with more pain and injury. And when you find yourself reliving an instant replay of your first fall on the motorcycle, you instinctively adjust the rear view mirror to focus on the last limb that has injured you. And if you don't learn to make the necessary changes, you will develop eyesight that sees none of the beauty of the mountain, only the limbs that have knocked you down. Thus, you create a perfect climate for the next limb that will surely knock you down.

The lesson in my little analogy is obvious: Those with unforgiving hearts are under the false assumption that they are correctly traveling forward, but they are actually like the driver moving down the road with his eyes firmly fixed on the rearview mirror. With eyes focused on the past, they unknowingly set the stage for future accidents. Over and over again, an unforgiving heart creates these self-fulfilling prophecies. While they may personally feel they are "not looking back, and refusing to let yesterday hold tomorrow hostage," they are only fooling themselves.[4]

I can't count the number of people who have come up to me after I have spoken of this concept to share similar experiences. In marriage, business, morality, or friends, they bear testimony of moving forward through life with eyes firmly fixed on the rearview mirror. Those with this problem live life like the movie *Groundhog Day*, in which every day is just a repeat of the day before. That is the future for those with an unforgiving heart.

One woman said to me, "I was fooled in my youth into marrying a man who turned out to be a monster. After years of agony, I divorced him. With a heart full of anger, I moved forward with my eyes firmly fixed on the rearview mirror. Five years later I married another man with the same problems. For the first time I understand how this could have happened."

Then she said something I found very intriguing, "Now, I understand that I was the victim only the first time. The second time I wasn't the victim; I was the fool."

I believe this is a battle we all must fight. Jeffrey R. Holland said, "The past is to be learned from but not lived in. We look back to claim the embers from glowing experiences but not the ashes. And when we have learned what we need to learn and have brought with us the best that we experienced, then we look ahead, we remember that faith is always pointed toward the future. . . . To be tied to earlier mistakes—our own or other people's is the worst kind of wallowing in the past from which we are called to cease and desist."[5]

This notion was brought home to me after my first heart attack. Months before this painful event, a very good doctor made a mistake in performing a procedure on me. Normally after this particular procedure the patient is able to resume regular activity within a few days. However, this was not the case for me. Although I did go back to work, I had a feeling that something was wrong. I just could not shake the idea that all was not well. I felt my strength slowly slipping from me.

My worst fears were realized in three months when I had a heart attack. This time another doctor went into my chest and corrected the problem, which placed me on the road to recovery. Within a short time, I went from a strong athlete to a depressed and bitter man. I could not get my thoughts off the fact that the first doctor had done this to me.

In his defense, he was a good man as well as a good doctor. He just overlooked something in my background, which if noticed, might have saved me a lot of grief. He was a well-respected doctor who gave his best effort in my behalf. For some reason, I needed someone to blame, and he was the best candidate.

As I tried to move forward with my life, my eyes were firmly fixed on the rearview mirror. And it was that doctor who stood out. Somehow, I needed my pain to be transferred to him. After all, wasn't this his fault?

Financially, we would be fine because I had great insurance that would support my family until I got back on my feet. But that wasn't the problem; the issue was that my pain was caused by someone else. Shouldn't he have to suffer for that?

As I became more and more consumed with this idea, the visitors who came to my home diminished. Those remaining few had the same thing in common—they wanted to talk about the terrible injustice which had been done to me and what I should do about it. They were drawn to me for the same reason I was drawn to them—we were all victims. They had their own stories, and we spent the time rehearsing the ways in which life had not been fair to us. It is amazing how the adversary can use fellowship against us when the topic of conversation is not uplifting. We were like sympathetic friends holding hands in a whirlpool that was taking us down. The old adage "there is strength in numbers" worked against us. When the cause is not just, the strength found in numbers is counterproductive.

Finally, I felt like I had reached the end of my ability to cope with the pain of my heart attack. In an interesting bit of rationalization, I made the decision that I was going to run as fast as I could until I was either going to get better or my heart would just explode. As I look back on it now, I'm not sure my attempt at running could even be interpreted as moving quickly. I'm not sure my "all out" effort would even be seen as jogging. It could best be described as "moving a little faster than walking," but it was the best I could do.

As I moved through orchards and trails near our home, I began to talk to my Heavenly Father. In the true spirit of seeing myself as a victim, I continually repeated the same plea: "Why did this happen to me?"

Somewhere in the mist of my pity party, my prayer became a bit more submissive. My words were changed from, "Why did this happen to me?" to "What am I to learn from this?"

Through it all, I ran until my chest felt like it was going to explode. The pain in my chest was matched only by the fatigue in my legs. Finally, I collapsed in the middle of an orchard at the base of the mountain. After a few minutes of recovery, I lifted up my weary head from the ground. Not more than twenty yards away from me was a deer gently grazing in the grass. As our eyes met, the thought came to me that even though I would have done him no harm, the deer sensed that in my weakened condition he was in no danger. For a long moment we studied each other; eventually, he just walked away.

Without kneeling I bowed my head in despair and said, "Heavenly Father, what would you have me learn from my heart attack?"

Just as clearly as if I had heard words, the message came into my wounded heart, "Let it go."

Immediately, I knew what the words were referring to. I received a distinct impression that my physical heart could not heal properly until my spiritual heart was healed through the process of forgiving those who had trespassed against me.

In those days, a commercial regularly seen on television appealed to those who had been injured through the negligence of another with these words: "One call, that's all!"

The words which had been delivered to my heart in the orchard echoed the same message; however, the call for me was to be made to a much higher authority than the lawyer on TV.

I poured out my soul, seeking for strength to do what my Heavenly Father asked of me, until there was nothing left to say. With all the energy I had left, I worked myself to my feet and migrated home. In the days that followed, as I concentrated on taking my eyes off the rearview mirror and looking to the future, the power to cope with each day came back to me. As my unforgiving heart began to heal, it was only natural that I began to feel no anger toward the doctor. I could see how his mistake could have happened. In fact, I could even see myself doing the same thing had I been in his shoes. My anger had been just a manifestation of the frustration that springs forth from an unforgiving heart. As I quit viewing my todays through the lens of yesterday, it was not difficult to let go of anger.

As a side note for those who have been sinned against to the point where legal action seems appropriate: Do not assume that in my encouraging forgiveness and nullifying anger, I am suggesting that the offender should not be accountable before the law. The manner in which this should be done is given by Richard G. Scott: "When anguish comes from evil acts of others, there should be punishment and corrective action taken, but the offended is not the one to initiate that action. Leave it to others who have that responsibility. Learn to forgive; though terribly hard, it will release you and open the way to newness of life. Time devoted by one injured to endure the offender is punished is time wasted in the healing process."[6]

While I did not feel the necessity of seeking legal action against the doctor, it would have been appropriate for my friend to participate in litigation against the drunk driver. Even if he had been asked to participate in prosecuting the drunk driver, his motive should not have been connected to anger and revenge. He still needed to forgive, for his own well-being, if for no other reason. The driver should have been required to suffer the legal consequences of the law he had broken—if for no other reason than to protect future victims. If my friend had chosen to participate in the legal process, he would have needed to move forward with a heart empty of revenge.

Emperor of the North

When I returned from my mission in England, I moved to Provo, Utah. It seemed to me that the options for finding my eternal companion would be greatly enhanced in that setting. As I dated over the next year, I met many wonderful young ladies and had some enlightening experiences.

On one occasion I asked an attractive girl to attend a movie with me. The name of the film was *The Emperor of the North.* In those days, movies were not rated, but if they were, this one probably would have been rated PG. The plot revolved around two men—one was the mean and rough conductor of a freight train, while the other was a hobo. The story evolved in such a way as to garner sympathy from the audience for the bum, and to encourage disdain for the conductor of the train. It accomplished this by showing the conductor of the train continually "bonk" freeloaders on the head with his hammer and then throw them off his moving train. The lack of integrity of the hobos regarding their efforts in obtaining something for nothing was easily forgotten as we viewed the far more revolting actions of the conductor of the train in making victims out of these homeless souls.

At the same time, the hero of the story was a fun loving, courageous hobo. As the script unfolded, it became easy for all in the theatre to develop a kinship with him. This set the perfect stage for the climax of the movie. The hero and the villain found themselves in hand to hand combat on a flat car of the moving train. The drama was enhanced when, through the magic of film, the combatants suddenly obtained an ax. The struggle went back and forth, until the hobo gained access to the weapon and swung it at the conductor of the train, where it found its mark.

That was the moment of triumph—when good finally conquered evil. A phrase must have been left off from the tablets given to Moses: "It's ok to kill the bad guys."

The entire theatre was filled with electricity as everyone in attendance was captured in the moment. Right at the instant of highest impact—when the audience's hearts were joined as one in full attention to the screen—my date abruptly stood and screamed. This was no ordinary yell. It was a high pitched, full-lunged female scream. She immediately sat down, with the prayer that no one would notice. That didn't happen. To say it dampened the moment for everyone else in attendance might be a bit of an understatement. In fact, I would not have been surprised if someone would have asked for their money back.

Within moments, the movie ended and everyone slowly migrated toward the exit. Even though my date was trying to go unnoticed, it was obvious that everyone was aware of her location as dirty looks and muffled murmurings were shot in our direction. If looks could kill, my date would have needed serious medical attention. Through it all, we sat silently, hoping we could just disappear. When the theatre was totally empty except for us, it became painfully obvious that it was time for us to get up from our hiding place. We departed slowly—silently into the night—until we climbed into the comfortable seclusion of my car. We had not spoken to each other since her ill-fated scream. Following a few minutes of travel, I broke the silence with something that lacked appropriate sensitivity, "What was that all about?"

Without looking at me, she humbly replied, "I've never seen anything like that before."

I didn't say anything, but my thoughts went something like, "Where have you been hiding? In a cave?"

Based on my exposure to life's realities, I found it hard to believe that a person had not seen anything like that before. I just shrugged my shoulders and continued through the rest of our date. In the weeks and months that followed, I saw a sweet gentleness in this girl that bore witness to the fact that mean-spirited movies and even violent sports were just not a part of her nature. As time went on, we were married in the Salt Lake Temple.

My experience with life up to that point had taught me that if you have a problem with a situation or a person, you lay out all your cards, as well as your emotions, on the table. If that meant that someone's feelings were wounded, then you try and put the pieces back together after the truth be told. I had believed that it was the honest thing to do, to express everything, even anger if you were really going to be true to the situation.

However, I quickly discovered in marriage that it was no fun to lay all my cards on the table—with all the negative emotions that accompany it—if my spouse wouldn't play along. I was willing to do my part, but she just wouldn't return fire. So I just quit trying to solve any problem we had between us with verbal and emotional fireworks, and my life (as well as our children's) have been blessed for it. In fact, the time she raised her voice in the movie theatre has never been matched in any conversation we have had in well over three decades of marriage. Added to the title of homemaker, she should be given the title of a peacemaker. The problems have been there, but her solution has never been delivered in the spirit of anger or revenge. Hers has always been a forgiving heart, and she has been as foreign to anger as oil is to water.

It has been easy for me to contrast her disposition to that of the Nephites when their nation came to its close. Mormon wrote to his son Moroni about this anger in the unforgiving hearts of his people: "Satan stirreth them up continually to *anger* one with another. . . . and when I speak the word of God with sharpness they tremble and *anger* against me" (Moroni 9:3-4, italics added). He continued, "I fear lest the Spirit of the Lord hath ceased striving with them" (Moroni 9:4).

Anyone who has been victimized by someone whose heart is filled with anger can bear witness (like Mormon) that the Spirit of the Lord and anger are normally not found in the same place.

There is a pronounced difference in the raising of one's voice in warning and raising the same voice in anger. In Lehi's dream of the Tree of Life, he spoke to his family "with a loud voice" in his invitation to come and partake of the fruit (1 Nephi 8:15). The "loudness" did not seem to be interpreted by his family as anger. The fact that he effectively gained his families attention "with a loud voice" might have to do with the fact that he used that level of volume so rarely. The same thing could be said of my wife.

As I count the blessings of my life, at the top would be that I have been sheltered by the love of my mother and later my wife—both of whom have no taste for anger. Just as anger is symptomatic of an unforgiving heart, a lack of it is evidence of genuine humility. As the world becomes filled with anger and revenge, those individuals who live with a sense of peace and control will surely be the jewels of the nations in which they reside.

It is not hard to see how genuine spirituality is foreign to those who explode like a balloon when someone rules them the wrong way. This type of member of the Church can easily become a "knife and fork" Mormon—eating the meal but lacking the ability to taste, always being where they are supposed to be, but not with the level of consecration needed to enjoy the flavor that comes with the companionship of the Holy Ghost. For this person there is no spiritual lengthening of the stride, and their activity in the Church is a spiritual masquerade. It is their loved ones who suffer—often behind closed doors as the mask comes off and anger is revealed. The member of the Church afflicted with anger may be a cultural Mormon but is not to be found with the same heart as those who are covenant members of the Gospel. Sporting events (even at BYU) and crowded freeways, or anything which quickly raises our stress levels reveal the hearts of people who have accepted anger as a way of life. It is one thing to lengthen our stride, but it is quite another to be blessed with the emotional control that allows us to effectively deal with the unexpected or the unplanned.

* For a further treatment of this subject see *Life Lessons from the Book of Mormon,* Christianson and Bassett, (Springville: Cedar Fort), 165–86.

Notes

1. Marion D. Hanks, in Conference Report, Oct. 1973, 15.
2. Neal A. Maxwell, "Repentance," *Ensign*, Nov. 1991, 32.
3. Jeffrey R. Holland, Brigham Young University Devotional, Jan. 13, 2009.
4. See Neal A. Maxwell, "Hope through the Atonement of Jesus Christ," *Ensign*, Nov. 1998, 63.
5. Jeffrey R. Holland, Brigham Young University Devotional, Jan. 13, 2009.
6. Richard G. Scott, "To Be Healed," *Ensign*, May 1994, 9.

chapter four

Optimism

Years ago as a seminary teacher in Phoenix, I was forcefully taught that our view of the world deals more with what is going on inside of us than what is happening around us. This lesson occurred on a typical Monday morning following a normal fast Sunday. However, that changed when into my office walked a female student I had only seen a few times that semester. Her life was the result of a series of choices that no good parent would wish for their teenage child. To say she had struggled spiritually might be considered an understatement. But this morning her attitude was not rebellious or even defensive. She was truly contrite and bright in her demeanor.

She stated that as she was sitting in testimony meeting, she felt something that she thought must be the Spirit. While it was unexpected, it just seemed to grow within her until she felt she had to go to the pulpit and express her feelings. She indicated that the impression only got stronger at the pulpit, and she heard herself saying that she knew the Church was true. Not wanting to lose that moment, she decided to come to seminary in hopes of staying close to that Spirit. She seemed to have a strong desire to make changes in her life for good. Leaving my office, she went into the classroom to read her scriptures until class started.

Within moments two other girls abruptly entered my office with a totally different perspective. These girls, by all accounts, would be considered active in the Church. They seldom missed meetings and were active in seminary in the sense that their attendance was good.

However, theirs was a different spirit than the one I felt in my office only a few minutes earlier. Like magpies sitting on the fence giving commentary regarding the world around them, their feelings were in unison. "Brother Bassett, you will never believe what happened in Church yesterday."

The sarcastic tone of their words indicated that the rest of their report wasn't going to be very uplifting. My fears proved to be right. "——got up and bore her testimony yesterday in church. The Spirit just left the meeting." Their toxic commentary continued, "What a hypocrite. With everything she has done, she shouldn't be allowed to stand at the pulpit."

With a huff, signaling that at least in their minds justice had been served, they turned on their heels and headed for the classroom, leaving me with an emptiness. Their words left me with the thought that what we say about others often reveals more about us than the person we are speaking about.

Two conversations—one filled with a witness of the Spirit and the second bearing witness that the Spirit had departed when the first girl stood at the pulpit. I was left with thoughts spinning in my own head as I pondered the contrast.

I have had the opportunity over the years to relate this story to many groups. Invariably, I ask them which testimony declared in my office that morning was correct regarding the presence of the Holy Ghost: The one that declared that the Spirit was strong or the one that stated the departure of the Spirit. What has surprised me is how often hands go up for one or the other. In actual fact, both testimonies were correct from their perspective. It is completely possible for one person to feel the Spirit, and in the same setting someone else is totally repulsed by the events before them. Anyone who has taught the gospel as a missionary or has been a teacher in a classroom setting can bear witness to that fact.

Elder Dennis B. Neuenschwander gave evidence to this point: "Many years ago when our boys were still very young, I made a remark at the dinner [table] regarding the excellence of our sacrament meeting and how much I had learned. Their response was a look that told me that they were not sure that we had even been in the same meeting. The difference between my experience and theirs was simply one of a little maturity and personal preparation."[1]

The Positive Lean

As an observer of people, I have been continually struck by the power of those who choose to see the world through the lens of optimism. I have been constantly reminded that what we think determines the world in which we live. This being true, then it would also be a fact that as we change, our world changes. The best evidence for this would be how the world and everything in it transforms during the process of conversion.

As I watched the most recent Olympics, I took special note of something that happened in the Track and Field Events. As the sprinters approached the finish line, a subtle yet profound thing occurred in each race. Only those runners who felt they had a chance to win threw their arms back and thrust forward their chests toward the tape that marked victory. Even though they were all participating in the same race, those whose hearts were filled with the expectation of success had what is called "the positive lean." In fact, it would have been out of place for the last place finisher to cross the finish line with his chest thrust forward being fully aware that he had no chance for victory. It occurs to me that this is true with life itself. For those who go through life without "the positive lean," time for them seems to be marked by a series of roadblocks designed (in their viewpoint) to hold them back. Their lives seem to be at the mercy of those things which annoy them. Their ability to overcome, even life's day to day obstacles, are severely compromised by their attitudes.

I was reminded of this truth many years ago in American Fork, Utah, when my children were young. I have enjoyed basketball throughout my life, and my children had witnessed me playing many times. We also spent many hours watching BYU basketball or the Jazz on TV. However, on these occasions when I attempted to shoot hoops with them, they didn't have the same focus and quickly lost interest. This seemed odd to me, because normally they loved doing things with me.

Then one day as I was driving by our bishop's house, I noticed he had taken off his old beat-up wooden backboard and hoop from over his garage door. Apparently, he had thrown it into a pile of grass in front of his house for the garbage man to pick up. I knocked on his door and received permission to take the backboard.

I then went behind our shed, which faced into the horse pasture and put it up as high as space would allow. The rim barely reached five feet from the ground, only half the height of a regulation hoop. As I nailed it up, I noticed the backboard was all bent with time and exposure to weather and had so much paint pealed off that it was hard to detect the original color. The rim, which once stood so ridged, had to be reinforced in order not to sag like an arthritic man in a wind storm. I looked to the ground recognizing that it was composed of uneven dirt, rocks, and weeds. I shrugged with the thought that I may have just constructed the most pathetic basketball court in miles.

I went to the grocery store and purchased a cheap rubber basketball out of a bin near the cash register. Returning home I announced to my children the grand opening of our new court. For the rest of the day, we played on that court. When night came I found a flood light and fastened it to a fence post. We played until Mom ordered us to come in and clean up for bed. We lived in that house for another year and that silly hoop often became the focal point of activity for my boys, as well as their friends. Contrast this with the fact that less than a block away were nice hoops overlooking level paved courts that went unused by the neighborhood children most of the time.

It didn't take a genius to figure out why my children shunned the quality basketball environment for the one that would rightly be called pathetic. It was due to the simple fact that the one behind our shed provided the greatest opportunity for success. The standard rim was too high, out of reach, and a consistent reminder of failure. However, their shots could reach the hoop tacked to the shed. Success is fun and even though they lost their share of games, at least they had a chance of reaching their objective. The basketball hoops at school were just a reminder that they were too small. Optimism, or what I've identified as the positive lean, is nothing more than an expectation of success—the bright hope that good things will come through work and perseverance.

I have seen many capable children grow to be much less than their potential, simply because they were raised in an environment that was not filled with optimism. Theirs became the self-fulfilled prophesy that great things will not happen to them. A "shadow on the brain" took away the positive lean and gave them the illusion that they were always shooting at a rim located just out of reach. Well-meaning parents, who love their children with all their hearts, sentence all but the strongest of their offspring to be less than they could be by creating an atmosphere in the home that stifles optimism.

The Three Types of Parenting

Having spent so much of my life around sports, I naturally see life through that lens. For example, I tend to divide parenting styles into three categories: the Referee, the Coach, and the Cheerleader.

In a basketball game, the referee's job is to blow the whistle, identify the guilty party, and dole out consequences. It is not his job to consider the feelings of the guilty party. However, it is his objective to make absolutely sure that justice is served. We will go a lifetime without seeing a referee blow his whistle at the end of a great play, just to draw the crowd's attention to a terrific performance by one of the players. While his job is essential to a good game, his input in the contest is often unappreciated when his whistle points out the negative behavior of a player we are rooting for.

On the other hand, the coach's job during the game revolves around giving instructions to the players. In doing this, it is often necessary for him to call a time out. It is his assignment to make plans for his team and make decisions that provide the best chance for success. The coach would be considered the teacher as opposed to the referee's role as a policeman.

Next we have the cheerleader, who has the singular role of providing encouragement and emotional reinforcement. They will still be seen screaming with enthusiasm even when the team is down fifty points and all is lost. When discouraged fans vacate the stands, and the team is watching the clock slowly wind down with the desire of escaping as soon as possible, the cheerleaders can still be seen bouncing around, doing whatever they can to get the crowd behind their hopelessly defeated team. I have never seen a cheerleader leave the game early because of discouragement or having lost faith in the team. If a game went on forever, it would be the cheerleader who could be given the title of the eternal optimist.

The transition to parenting from the Referee, the Coach, and the Cheerleader is not a difficult task. There are certainly positives, as well as negatives in each of the three. We can see the need for the Referee parent when discipline and consequences are required. We can also see that if this is the dominant parental style, then consistent negative reinforcement will drive children from their parents and into the hands of those who might carefully lead them to destruction.

When the Referee parent has become the dominant style, these words by Brigham Young may be well to consider: "It has been the custom of parents to break the will [of their children] until it is weakened, and the noble, God-like powers of the child are reduced to a comparative state of imbecility and cowardice."[2] It is in this extreme setting that the virtue of discipline becomes a vice.

When one is a parent, he or she is also a Coach or a teacher. This cannot be delegated, and we can never underestimate the value of great parental teaching in the home. The only negative aspect to correct instruction in the home is when it becomes overbearing, or when parents reinforce to the child that they the parents are all knowing and that any instruction outside the home is not to be valued. This kind of parenting often achieves the same negative result as the Referee—children are always looking over their own shoulder in a posture of self-preservation.

However, it is not hard to see the advantages of Cheerleader parents who are constantly rooting for their children. When this style turns against them is when they become blinded into the false assumption that their children are somehow better than other children and are therefore perfect and make no mistakes. The parent with this flaw finds it impossible to be the Referee when discipline and justice are required. They also find little need to be the diligent teacher-Coach because, after all, their children are already perfect.

As a gospel instructor for many years in a variety of settings, I have made many conclusion that may surprise you. I have taught long enough that my students are now the children of my original students, and it won't be too long before I may be seeing their grandchildren. My observation is that with the breakdown of the family, all three of these categories of parenting have weakened considerably. But the category most surprisingly affected, even in active LDS homes, is the Cheerleader. Perhaps it is because more young people are behaving in ways that cause their parents to have less optimism toward them. Perhaps it is because with both parents working, no one consistently nurtures the children. Maybe it is just a reflection of the world as a whole.

I don't pretend to have all the answers. But this much I do know: The role of the parent that must always be in place is the Cheerleader. Even the best of gospel instruction in the home is undermined when the parents stop believing in their children. And all that remains is the Referee parent, who creates a kind of police-state—focusing on punishment for bad behavior, as opposed to reward for correct behavior.

As parents we must be the occasional Referee, and the consistent teacher, but 100 percent of the time—even when we are performing within the first two roles—we must be the Cheerleader. Would the prodigal son have ever considered coming home if he were not totally confident that his father was a Cheerleader? Would he have risked the journey home if his father was only the Referee?

Being the Cheerleader is not to neglect the other two roles; it is, however, to always be the optimist regarding our children. This becomes challenging when their behavior becomes destructive to themselves or to others. The Cheerleading parent is not necessarily a "ra ra" specialist, but one whose obedient life is reflected in his love and optimism toward his children. In fact, the Coach role can easily be misinterpreted by the children as a Referee, without the constant emotional support of the Cheerleader role.

These words of President Joseph F. Smith describe the Cheerleading parent: "Govern the children, not by . . . bitter words or scolding, but by affection and by winning their confidence. If you can only convince your children that you love them, that your soul goes out to them for their good, that you are their truest friend, they, in turn, will place confidence in you and will love you and seek to do your bidding and to carry out your wishes with your love. But if you are selfish, unkindly to them, and if they are not confident that they have your entire affection, they will be selfish, and will not care whether they please you or carry out your wishes or not, and the result will be that they will grow wayward, thoughtless and careless. . . . If children are defiant and difficult to control, be patient with them until you can conquer by love, and you will have gained their characters as you please."[3]

On another occasion this same Prophet stated: "Prove to them that you do love them by your every word or act to them. . . . However wayward they might be . . . when you speak . . . to them, do it not in anger, do it not harshly, in a condemning spirit. Speak to them kindly; . . . weep with them if necessary. . . . Use no lash and no violence . . . approach them with reason, with persuasion and love unfeigned. . . . Our children are like we are; we couldn't be driven. . . . Men are not in the habit of being driven; they are not made that way. . . . You can't force your boys, nor your girls into heaven. You may force them to hell, by using harsh means in the efforts to make them good. . . . The man that will be angry at his boy, and try to correct him while he is in anger, is the greatest fault; he is more to be pitied and more to be condemned than the child who has done wrong. You can only correct your child in love, in kindness, by love unfeigned, by persuasion, and reason."[4]

To me President Smith's words became the defining moment for optimism as a parent. It is so easy to give our misbehaving children what we think they deserve, but it is so difficult to have the wisdom and the discipline to also give them what they need. To give them genuine love when they are not lovable, or even open to the possibility, may be the defining moment of parenting.

Many years ago, one of my children went through an extremely rocky time in his life. I must admit there was a time or two (in my weaker moments) in which I wanted to clobber him and give him the full measure of justice. With 20/20 hindsight, I easily saw that the Referee role within me in full bloom. I felt that by staying in the Referee role I would have his attention, and then the Coach parent could take over and show him the error of his ways.

I had just enough discipline to recognize when my anger was about to take over and that I needed to wait for my emotions to die down before I did something I might regret. I decided to pray, fast, and attend the temple before I acted. The feelings I had following my temple attendance were totally unexpected. As I sat pondering on what to do, these thoughts came to me, and I knew they were not my thoughts: "A positive attitude may not make things better at the moment, but a negative attitude will surely make things worse."

This proved to be my role in the situation. I became aware that for the moment I may not be a part of the solution, but by being too forceful, I could definitely become a part of the problem. I knew that in my present frame of mind of anger, I would overreact in the role of Referee or Coach. Yet, there was no way I wanted to be a Cheerleader. In my mind, that was the last thing he deserved and the last thing I wanted to be. But as I focused on staying the course with a positive attitude, I became part of the long range solution, rather than connected to the immediate problem. After a short time, I appropriately took on the role of the Referee and the Coach, but neither one of these would have been accepted by my son had I not immediately taken on the role of the Cheerleading parent as well. I was reminded that optimism as a parent can be the hardest thing to keep consistent when dealing with a misbehaving child.

A Cheerleading Teacher

Back in the 1970s, my first assignment as a full-time seminary teacher was in Phoenix, Arizona, at East High School. I was asked to replace an excellent teacher who had quit in the middle of the school year. The seminary was a room built on the back of the home we lived in, and was located across the street from the school. The first devotional I heard as a teacher was from a girl who announced that she was pregnant, to which she received a rousing ovation from her fellow students. A few days into my assignment, I excused myself to run into the house to grab a piece of chalk. Moments later I came back into the room to discover that some of the ping-pong paddles were broken and the balls were mashed on the floor. Looking at the guilty party, I asked simply, "Why?" To which the young man replied, "Why not?"

Many of the student's three-ring binders, as well as the scriptures, had their covers deliberately torn off. Graffiti was scribbled throughout the books. The book cases which housed the student materials were marred with irreverent whittlings. This was my first introduction to full-time seminary instruction. I must admit that during my initial week as a teacher, I did little to get things going in the right direction. In fact, my lessons were so poor that the students had little reason to pay attention. At the end of each school day, I buried myself in preparation, but the result was that the next day was no better than the previous. My discouragement began to mount to the point that I considered following in the footsteps of my predecessor and leaving the job to someone else.

Knowing they loved their former teacher, I asked the class what they remembered most about him. They said that they would never forget the day they finally "got him." Upon further inquiry, they revealed that no one would play the piano, so he had to play records of the hymns, to which few of the students would participate in the singing anyway. They said one day he just snapped and ran over to the record player. After removing the record, he flung it like a Frisbee just above their heads until it smashed against the front wall. They thought that was so funny. I reminded them that he had been a great teacher who had been with them for almost four years, and that was what they would remember most? They confirmed.

That was it! That was my first defining moment as a teacher! I made a commitment then and there that I would never express myself in a negative way. I would be optimistically enthusiastic, no matter what they did to me. I knew that I wasn't a good teacher, yet. But I believed, with hard work, that it would happen over time. Until I got to that point, I could always be positive and express myself with optimism.

From then on, each time I shook their hands, I looked in their eyes and smiled with all the love I could bring up from my soul. Even though my lessons were weak, I gave them with hopeful optimism. I stood before the class and promised that I would be their number one fan—that I would be at their games and activities, and I would love them second only to my own family. Most of all, I would never speak to their faces or behind their backs in any way that would undermine my love for them. Something magical happened. It didn't even occur over a period of time—it happened immediately. Seminary was great, and I never enjoyed myself so much! It has been three decades since that first week and I still get regular phone calls and letters from many of those students. I'm actually teaching some of their children right now in college.

I'm wise enough to know that the level of teaching in the classroom didn't improve drastically that first year, but I made a connection that began with optimism and a positive commitment to the lives of that group of young people. Because of this, those students made up for what I lacked as a teacher, and the Spirit of the Lord did the rest. That group of young people were the same as the youth of today—they desperately needed adults who loved them and believed in them. I'm sure that very few of the lessons I taught will be remembered, but they will always remember that I believed in them and their potential to do good.

After a few years of teaching in Phoenix, I was transferred to Provo High School in Utah. By this time, I was confident in my abilities as a teacher, and did not suffer the same anxiety going into Provo High Seminary, as I did beginning at East. I knew I needed to come into class that first day with a great lesson, because none of these students had any frame of reference for me as a teacher. The first fifteen minutes of class were great, and I was confident that everything would turn out fine. I felt like the Lone Ranger delivering my silver bullet lesson. Suddenly, a young man entered from the back. He seemed to have perfected a role that the students were immediately drawn to. His disrespectful comedy routine removed the class from my grasp, and I didn't quite get the students back before the bell rang. He apparently had this act mastered because he exited the scene before I had a chance to nab him. I didn't want my initial confrontation with him to be on the phone so I decided to visit with him the next day.

If it is possible for two days to be carbon copies of each other, then that is what happened. He orchestrated his entrance and exit perfectly, with his classroom performance coming off beautifully. It was not hard to see who was in control. I may have been the teacher, but he was definitely the emergent leader of those students. After the students emptied the classroom, I was left alone with my thoughts. My initial feelings of discouragement were replaced with indignation toward this young man. "Who does he think he is?" was soon followed by, "I'll fix him good."

I rushed into my office and quickly dialed his home phone. He would not get another opportunity to ruin one of my classes, because he would not be in another one of my classes. He was soon to be history. I justified these negative feelings with a self-righteous desire to save the rest of the class. I felt like Nephi when he picked up Laban's sword to cut off his head. This time it would be me cutting off this disrespectful punk from the rest of the class. I was so full of what I thought was righteous indignation, that I could almost hear the angel in 1 Nephi speaking to me, "It is better that one . . . [student] should perish than that a . . . [class] should dwindle and perish in unbelief" (1 Nephi 4:13). It's so easy not to see clearly when we are out of control. Especially when we can back it up with scripture!

What happened to that humble, insecure teacher in Phoenix? Where was the guy who had little to give but optimism and belief in each student? Slowly, over a period of time he had been replaced with a teacher who was so confident in his ability to deliver in the classroom, that no one, not even those he was to serve, would get in the way.

My thoughts were interrupted by a kind and gentle middle-aged female voice on the other end of the phone. Nearly interrupting his mother I said, "Is ________ your son?" My tone was more accusation than respectful.

Her reply was sweet, almost apologetic, like she was expecting some bad news.

The sweet and gentle manner in which she spoke seemed to bring me to my senses. I suddenly remembered that teacher in Phoenix and how he spoke to and about his students. I heard myself saying, "My name is Brother Bassett. I am your son's seminary teacher."

I hesitated knowing that I would have to pay for what I said next. "I just want you to know how much I appreciate having your son in my class. I think he is great."

I couldn't believe I had said that! Surely, I had to rephrase things to reflect the truth!

Before, I could speak, there were soft gentle sobs coming through the phone. These were interrupted with, "My son is a senior in high school, and in all the years he has been in school, this is the first positive thing I have heard from one of his teachers." She hesitated just long enough to gather her emotions. "I love my son, and I will cherish your words forever."

Now what was I to do?

She thanked me once again and hung up.

A funny thing happened next—I loved her son, too. Suddenly, in my mind I was back in Phoenix, not knowing what I would do next, but with a firm determination that I was going to be optimistically enthusiastic. I didn't know how, but some way, things were going to work out.

The next day, I was in the classroom ten minutes before the class started setting up the chalkboards for my lesson. In walked the young man who had given me so much grief. His was not the cocky step of the student I had witnessed the first two days of class. He was tentative and unsure of himself. I waited for him to speak first. He approached me and stuck out his right hand that I accepted enthusiastically.

Looking into my face, he said, "I don't know why you said what you did to my mother yesterday." He glanced to the floor and mused, "You and I both know you probably should have said something else."

I hugged him and told him that I was aware of how much courage it took for him to do what he just did. He asked what he could do to repay my kindness. I surprised him by asking if he would be my class president.

He was great in that role for the entire semester. The next semester brought new classes with new students. I heard within a short time, he was creating problems in his new class. It wasn't long before he was out of seminary, and in a short period, he was no longer a part of the school. With all my efforts I could not find him through the rest of the year.

The next year I began working on my graduate studies and teaching religion at BYU. John Beck, the principal of the Provo Seminary, asked me to speak for the students at a Sunday fireside in a nearby chapel.

The fireside was going great, and it was such fun to be with so many students I had served while at Provo Seminary. In the middle of my speech, I glanced to my left. The door that separated the pulpit area from the hallway had a small window in it. That window was filled with the face of the young man I had grown to love so much. He smiled, as did I. Seeing him again was the best thing which could have happened to me that evening. His heart is tied to mine in the same way that my heart is forever welded to the select few who believed in me when I was young and fragile.

I am reminded of the power of enthusiastic optimism when genuinely directed toward a young person. I wonder how much of the love we feel toward our youth is not accepted because it either goes unexpressed or is delivered in an atmosphere that is not filled with enthusiastic optimism.

Outlooks That Hinder

As a teacher for the past thirty years, I have tried to encourage my students to feel optimistic about themselves as well as their futures. For those who have been raised in a negative family environment, it takes a lot of hard work over an extended period of time to lift themselves beyond their crippling thoughts. I try to encourage them to look within themselves and root out those personal outlooks that destroy optimism. The following are some of the personal outlooks I have witnessed which hinder their progress. I would invite the reader to look deep within themselves to see if you reflect any of these crippling perspectives.

- I am valuable when I am accepted by others.
- I don't put myself in uncomfortable circumstances or situations where I might fail.
- The world should be fair.
- Life should be easier.
- People should act the way I want them to.
- If I had more money, I'd be happy.
- If I were out of school, I'd be happy.
- If someone loved me, I'd be happy.
- If I were married, I'd be happy.
- If I lived somewhere else, I'd be happy.
- If those I love aren't happy, I am a failure.
- I can't overcome past events in my life.
- I can't overcome cravings.
- I am powerless because of my genetic chemistry.
- Actions and attitudes of other people make me sad.
- I did bad things so I am a bad person.
- I can't change.
- People are basically mean.
- I am controlled by my environment.
- I can't trust people.
- I am good only when I look good.

Our attitudes create a self-fulfilling prophecy that becomes the blueprint for our lives. Dr. Phillip Roos wrote:

> When you go to a multi-screen theatre, you select a movie that will help you to feel what you want to feel. If you want to cry and feel sad, you will select a "tearjerker." If you want to laugh, you will go to a comedy. Likewise, you can select the internal movies you view. . . . If you want to intensify anger, guilt, shame, and\or depression . . . you will choose to select movies that will reinforce your negative judgment of self . . . .
>
> Suppose that you have just completed an abominable game of golf, and you tell yourself: "I really . . . [messed] that up! Once again, I didn't do it well enough. The harder I try, the worse I get. I keep failing, and I guess that I'm just a failure!" This internal expression . . . generates shame ("I'm a failure") and contributes to depression. . . .
>
> Unfortunately, people who specialize in anger have impressive [internal] movie collections of examples of other people's wrongdoings and few—if any—movies of being treated well by others. People who specialize in depression, on the other hand, have massive movie collections of personal inadequacies and misdeeds and few—if any—movies of personal successes and validation by other people. It may be difficult, therefore, for such people to select positive [internal] movies, since they may not have collected them."[5]

A Cup That Is Overflowing

There are certain ways of expressing ourselves that have become acceptable in society but are difficult for me to buy into. For example: "Is your cup half full or half empty?"

While I appreciate the sentiment I just can't embrace the mind-set. For example: If I had just finished a hard day of physical labor in the hot sun, and someone asked me if I wanted a tall cold glass of water, I would obviously be interested. If they proceeded to pour me half a glass of refreshing water, I wouldn't look at it and comfort myself with the thought that, "Well, my container is half full as opposed to half empty." Half is half!

I don't want to go through my life playing mind games with myself. I would turn to the fellow pouring the water and say, "I would like mine filled to overflowing." Not to be demanding or ungracious, but as an expression of the joy of fully participating in what is placed before me. If there was plenty of water for everyone, I would like my glass to be complete. By this, I don't mean to be pushy or overbearing, but truly joyfully optimistic.

I had a friend when I was a student at BYU who was the most optimistic person I had ever known. I served with him in the mission field, so I was quite aware of his attitude. Everything that came from his voice was positive, thoughtful, and optimistic. If someone were to say something pessimistic, he would just smile and say something like, "I could have gone all day without hearing that."

The singles scene at BYU is similar to any other campus, in that, first impressions have a great deal to do with appearances. That is what is so surprising about my friend. Without a lengthy description of his physical appearance, let me tactfully state he was not the poster child for the successful dating campaign. Yet, he was surrounded by the fairest flowers of the opposite sex. I knew it wasn't his rippling muscles or wavy hair, because he had little of either. However, his success with people, all the way from England to BYU, could not be denied. He always looked for the best in people and situations, and he was fearless in expressing himself with optimism. The perfect illustration is the day he was walking through a parking lot on campus and an attractive coed walked past him. The two had never laid eyes on each other before that day. In fact, she had not noticed his passing, but he was fully aware of everything around him.

She was at least ten feet past him when he turned to get her attention. "Excuse me, I don't mean to interrupt you, but I just wanted to tell you that you really look great." After a short pause, he concluded with, "Have a nice day."

That was it. Only those who knew him well would accept the truth that he had no ulterior motive—he was just being himself, truthfully optimistic. It was just his way.

He then continued toward his destination.

However, she just stood there in stunned disbelief. She gathered herself enough to say in a voice loud enough for him to hear some twenty feet away, "That's it! That's all you have to say?" Gathering up her courage, she asked, "Aren't you going to ask me out?"

He walked toward her, and after some light conversation, made a date. About a year later, the two were married in the temple. He is living proof that a prince does not have to look the part to be charming. He was Prince Charming because he optimistically focused on the bright side of everything, and that rare quality is a magnet that all good people are drawn to.

The Rustmobile

I've never considered how many memorable experiences we have had with old cars until I started writing this book. While my son Spencer was serving his mission in Iowa, finances were a little tight for us. The drive to work each day was eighty-four miles round trip, and it became obvious that I would need to find alternative transportation.

My friend Wynn Wilkes happened to mention that he had a Volkswagen Rabbit that was currently engulfed by weeds in a field behind his house. He said that it ran okay when he placed it there a few years earlier, and anyone was welcome to have it. He also said that it wasn't very pretty, and he had tried to give it away many times to people who had transportation problems, but after taking a glance at it, they had chosen to walk.

My circumstances were such that his offer felt like a gift from heaven. After all, no one had ever accused me of being very stylish in what I wore or drove.

I poured a little bit of gas into the tank as well as in the carburetor and tried to jump-start the Rabbit. To my surprise it fired right up. With very little work, I drove that car to work for almost two years. It was so old and weathered, we weren't quite sure what color it was, so we just called it the "Rustmobile." It had so many wonderful features including the fact that I could look through open parts of the floor on the driver's side to make sure the road was safely moving along underneath me. While the windshield wipers worked, they had a wonderful quirk of not touching the glass if I drove the vehicle over sixty miles per hour. They would just wave in the most friendly fashion to the cars passing by. I'm just estimating about the speed being sixty miles per hour because the speedometer didn't function real well. The radio didn't work either, and it took a while for the heat to get going on those cold winter trips to work. Of course, it didn't really matter that the radio was silent because the car made so much noise going down the road that I would not have heard it anyway. Even though it didn't pollute, I'm amazed that it passed inspection. But, it did get great gas mileage, and with no car payment, it helped us pay the bills during my son's mission.

One morning, the freeway traffic coming into work was unusually bad, and I feared that I would be late to an 8:00 AM class I was to teach. I try to always look on the bright side of things, but the situation wasn't looking very cheery as traffic trudged along. Finally, I exited the freeway and got to the campus where I work. I felt, with a little bit of luck, I would make it to class a minute or two early. As I approached the faculty parking lot at the Orem Institute of Religion, I noticed through my rearview mirror the flashing lights of a campus policeman. To make matters worse, the students were exiting the building from the previous class and were very aware of me, the Rustmobile, and the policeman.

As I pulled into my parking spot, I felt like the whole world was watching the policeman get out of his car with his ticket book in hand. When he reached me, he looked at the car with a bit of a smirk and said, "Are you aware that you were speeding?"

With no hope of avoiding justice, I replied with as much optimism as I could sum up, "You've got to be kidding. I thought the only way this piece of junk could exceed the speed limit was to fall off a cliff."

His stern countenance gave way to a hearty laugh. Removing his sunglasses, he stepped back to take another glance at the car. With a big smile he said, "I see what you mean."

He then took his ticket book and slapped me in the shoulder with it, and said, "Be a little more careful next time."

I can't think of very much in this story that might set an example for any young person reading this book. However, I would like to illustrate one thing. While I was making no attempt to avoid justice, I will state that it was my efforts of accepting the situation with as much optimism as I could that placed the officer and me on the same page. I'm sure grateful he had a sense of humor, too!

A Prophetic Kind of Optimism

President Gordon B. Hinckley will be remembered for many remarkable things that happened in the Church during his tenure as Prophet. The building of temples, the growth of the Church as a whole, the humanitarian efforts, and the expansion of educational opportunities will all be a part of his legacy. But like so many others, I will always remember his great optimism. The following is just a flavor of marvelous light of hope that he radiated even during some very dark times:

> Spare yourselves from the indulgence of self-pity. It is always self-defeating. Subdue the negative and emphasize the positive.[6]

> I see so many good people everywhere—and there's so much good

in them. And the world is good. Wonderful things are happening in the world. This is the greatest age in the history of the earth. . . . We have every reason to be optimistic. Tragedy is around yes. Problems everywhere, yes. . . . You can't, you don't, build out of pessimism or cynicism. You look with optimism; work with faith, and things happen.[7]

I just go forward on the assumption that everything works out.[8]

I am an optimist! . . . With that frame of reference, my plea is that we stop seeking out the storms and enjoy more fully the sunlight. . . . What I am suggesting is that we have had missing from our society a buoyant spirit of optimism. What I am suggesting is that we turn from the negativism that so permeates our culture and look for the remarkable good in the land and times in which we live . . . that optimism replace pessimism; that uncertainty and worry be pushed aside by an enduring feeling of hope. . . . We are creatures of our thinking. We can talk ourselves into defeat, or we can talk ourselves into victory. . . . We all tend do worry about the future. And yes, there may be lean days ahead for many of us. But we must not despair or give up. We must look for the sunlight through the clouds. . . . Criticism and pessimism . . . spread a shroud of gloom over entire nations. We must resist partaking of the spirit of our times. We need rather to look for the good all about us.[9]

There is good all around us—if we only look for it. . . . look for the great good among those with whom we associate and live . . . speak of one another's virtues and positive qualities more than we speak of another's faults, that optimism replace pessimism. . . . Who wants to be around someone who is always forecasting doom? Who wants to be fed a steady diet of the negative? Optimism, on the other hand, and looking on the bright side, refreshes everyone. In my ninety-plus years, I have learned a secret. I have learned that when good men and good women face challenges with optimism, things will always work out! Truly, things always work out! Despite how difficult circumstances may look at the moment, those who have faith and move forward with a happy spirit will find that things always work out.[10]

A story about President Hinckley that my dear friend Jonn Claybaugh shared with me further illustrates the need for simple day to day optimism:

On May 14, 1992, I was in I was invited, along with nine others,

> to take an informal tour of the Salt Lake Temple interior. We were escorted by the temple recorder as he showed us various rooms on each of the several floors.
>
> One of the highlights was to be allowed into the fourth-floor dressing room of the First Presidency. This is where the members of the First Presidency change into their temple clothing for their weekly Thursday morning meetings with the Quorum of the Twelve. This small room is adjacent to the Council Room of the First Presidency and the Twelve, near the northwest corner of the temple.
>
> In this room are three beautiful hardwood wardrobe closets, used [at that time] by President Ezra Taft Benson and his counselors, Gordon B. Hinckley and Thomas S. Monson. Each closet had a brass name plate attached, and as I read their names I was surprised to see that President Hinckley's last name was spelled without the letter c. I said to the temple recorder, 'Is it possible that they have misspelled President Hinckley's last name?' He walked over and looked at the name plate and with a look of disbelief on his face replied, 'I can't believe it! I've never noticed that before. It will be changed tomorrow!'
>
> What is remarkable about this story is that by this time in 1992, President Hinckley had been a member of the First Presidency for almost eleven years (since July 1981) and presumably had been using this same dressing room and closet during that entire time. Of course a person would notice the misspelling of his own name, and could expect that a person reaching this level of leadership could at least have his name spelled correctly. But obviously President Hinckley had never mentioned this to anyone, for if he had, it surely would have been corrected immediately.

This story is consistent with President Hinckley's life. True optimism hasn't the time to be offended by the mistakes of others. The variable which allowed this kind of behavior is the understanding that he was involved in a much greater cause than himself. Capturing this same vision allows us to "cease to find fault one with another" (D&C 88:124). President Hinckley's lack of initiative in pointing out the error in his name plate reminds me of the message on the Bulletin Board for the Salt Lake Temple ordinance workers in 1990: "Correction sometimes may be more offensive to the Lord than the error being corrected." The life of this great Prophet, as well as the life of President Thomas S. Monson, exemplifies the positive lean of optimism that separates all true servants of the Lord from the preoccupation with themselves.

Everything Works Out, So Have a Good Laugh

President Hinckley's attitude toward life and how to approach life's problems had a profound impact on me. It proved to be valuable to me about six years ago when I suffered my second heart attack. As I was prepping for surgery, I felt as if along with all the pain I was going through, a cloud of despair rested itself over me and initiated the darkest of emotional weather conditions. I felt myself losing hope, and fear became my closest companion. In an effort to fight against this destructive mentality, I tried to hold fast to something which might lift me above this dark cloud. I had been studying President Hinckley's talks, so my mind fixed itself on these words by the Prophet, "Go forward on the assumption that everything works out."

It may seem odd, but as I continually repeated this phrase I felt hope coming back to me. While they were preparing me for the operating room, I began visiting with the doctors and the nurses and found myself offering them encouragement. I also thought of my fellow teachers and secretaries at the Orem Institute of Religion. I wanted to do everything I could to lighten their emotional load. So I asked a nurse to get me a pen and paper, and I started writing everything about my predicament which I thought was funny. I entitled it, "News from the ER." As crazy as it seems, I was chuckling all the way to the operating table. When I awoke from the surgery and the affects of the anesthesia began to wear off, I continued to write. I read the jokes and stories to the doctors, nurses, as well as my family, and we had a few good laughs. A number of people actually got caught up in the excitement and gave me some great ideas. I sent the material to a faculty meeting, where I am told that they had a chuckle.

Without trying to bore the reader, here are a couple of the jokes. This one actually happened to a friend of mine and I just adapted it to my situation: "Knowing that I would be lying on a rock hard, frozen, stiff operating table, wearing ghetto lingerie in mixed company made me about as comfortable as croutons on a cow pie. To make matters worse I discovered that the surgeon was a University of Utah football fan. So, I had the nurse who shaved me write an X over my heart in blue felt pen and the following discourse on my belly! 'Under the X lies my heart. It's not the end zone so you ought to be able to find it.' "

Here are just a few more: "I knew the day of my heart surgery was not going to be a total success when I came into the admissions room and sat down next to a guy wearing a tie-dye shirt and bell-bottom trousers. His facial expression looked like he was hung over from the sixties. Trying to be polite, I said, 'Is this chair saved?' He slowly looked in my direction. With glazed eyes and a semi-conscious disposition he slowly said, 'No, but I'm praying for it.' "

"Just before I blacked out from the anesthesia, I had the thought that half of all Americans have probably failed math and the other 2/3 don't really care."

This next one, I adapted from a story my brother Rob related to me: "After returning home from my heart attack, I sat alone, downstairs, deep in despair. I felt my world was closing in on me and I began to question whether or not I would pull through. Suddenly, things started looking up when my nose caught hold of the sweet aroma of chocolate chip cookies. The thought occurred to me that I do have something to look forward to—the taste of chocolate chip cookies. Maybe I will survive after all! It took all my energy to drag myself upstairs. I couldn't believe my eyes—there were four trays of my favorite cookies. I may not die of a heart attack, but there may be the possibility that I could eat myself to death. Just as my hand found it's way to a cookie and halfway to my mouth, our good neighbor lady leaped into the kitchen. With the reflexes of a cat, she snatched the cookie from my hand and said, 'Don't eat that, we'll be needing all the cookies for the funeral!' "

The whole time I was in the hospital, I looked for funny things I could write down. By focusing on that positive activity, I wrote around three or four pages of jokes. In that environment, I was safe—the employees of the hospital only knew me as a patient, and I slipped into that relationship until (in an odd way) I felt at home.

Within a few days, I was excused from the hospital and sent to my real home. Immediately, I became very anxious because no one, including me, knew where I fit in. Even though my house was filled with love and concern, I felt strangely out of place in my own home. I have always been a very physical person—but I had no ability to do any type of work or play. I could tell that my family, as well as my friends, were trying to make an adjustment to the new Doug Bassett. I could feel there was one question on everyone's mind that no one dared express out loud: "Are you ever going to be yourself again?"

Throughout my adult life, I have been a fitness nut and regularly lifted weights. Following my heart attack, in the space of less than two weeks,

I had lost thirty pounds. One of my friends looked at me for the first time and announced, "There stands Doug Bassett—a shadow of himself!" I must admit it took all my energy to laugh at that one.

I won't have to die to witness the surreal gaze the mourners will cast in the direction of my open casket. I'm convinced it will be just like the initial expression I saw on the faces of those who visited me at home following my exit from the hospital. As I continually rehearsed my condition with well wishers, I could feel myself falling into a dark emotional hole. I could see that I was affecting their mood as well. Unlike the hospital, I was no longer in control of the emotional atmosphere. So I came up with a plan to transform the disposition of the mourners in another direction. Maybe I could never be the old Doug Bassett, but that didn't mean the new me wasn't without worth.

I decided to use humor to let the visitors realize that I may have had a heart attack but a heart attack didn't have me. I wanted them to know that at this point in my life, I would much rather be *seen* than *viewed.*

The town of Mona was experiencing a change that was painful for all us "good ole boys" who loved the rural lifestyle and the country ways that had always been ours. The community was experiencing subdivisions, sidewalks, and an influx of urban cowboys, which some of the good ole boy's believed didn't know the difference between a cow pie and an apple pie. A tension was in the town that made the newcomers feel less welcome than they deserved. You could even feel it at church.

So I thought I would write up something called "The 20 Reasons You Might Want to Move to Mona." I used this to defuse the mood that had accompanied the visits from concerned friends. I lightheartedly counseled my visitors that if they could identify any people who reflected at least three of the twenty items, then they might want to invite them to move into our fair town.

I then read the following:

1. If your parents had corn bread for their wedding cake . . . you might want to move to Mona.
2. If anyone in your family has ever spelled farm E-I-E-I-O . . . you might want to move to Mona.
3. If, when you got sick as a child, your parents called the vet . . . you might want to move to Mona.
4. If you've ever tried to order a John Wayne movie from Church

Distribution . . . you might want to move to Mona.

5. If you think there should be at least one country western ballad in the hymnal . . . you might want to move to Mona.
6. If your grandpa takes off his cowboy hat and his forehead is as white as a ghost, and his hair sticks up like a chia pet . . . you might want to move to Mona.
7. If you've ever done the wave in Church . . . you might want to move to Mona.
8. If you've ever done mouth to mouth resuscitation on a horse . . . you might want to move to Mona.
9. If your family car has ever been used in a demolition derby . . . you might want to move to Mona.
10. If you think cats land on their feet just because you toss them wrong . . . you might want to move to Mona. (That's just wrong! I apologize to cat lovers everywhere. I have two cats and would never throw them.)
11. If your grandpa's headstone reads, "Get'r Done". . . you might want to move to Mona.
12. If your grandma uses Bengay as perfume . . . you might want to move to Mona.
13. If your standard of living improves when you go camping . . . you might want to move to Mona.
14. If you've ever whistled at a woman in Church . . . you might want to move to Mona.
15. If you think the literal translation of "It came to pass" is "Oh, my heck". . . you might want to move to Mona.
16. If all the best dressed men in your family picture look as uncomfortable in their suits as Jabba the Hut does in a speedo . . . you might want to move to Mona.
17. If your dad has more hair in his nose than on his head . . . you might want to move to Mona.
18. If you've ever closed a meeting by saying, "We're burning daylight" . . . you might want to move to Mona.
19. If you've ever chest-bumped the Bishop . . . you might want to move to Mona.
20. If your belt buckle has ever been used as a hub cap . . . you might want to move to Mona.

After sharing the "20 Reasons" with my friend Ron Beatty from Mona, he told me that his wife didn't like camping because of the loss of "convenience."

So he put a toilet seat on the back of his four wheeler with an accompanying curtain for privacy. This certainly qualifies as another reason to move to Mona.

I found that laughter was the perfect way to get off the uninspiring subject of my health and just get back to being alive. I truly wanted all my visitors to leave my house with their hearts a little lighter than when they knocked on my door. For me, nothing is more depressing than dwelling on the negative state of my body. It seems the older we get the more we have a need to speak of bodily functions. A little light was brought into a very dark time for me, just by trying with every ounce of energy I had to reflect the optimism of President Hinckley's words: "Go forward on the assumption that everything works out." True to this Prophet's words, things have worked out.

I have tried to organize my thinking in such a way that develops a personal perspective which builds optimism. I claim no originality in what has become my "personal attitude guidelines." I have just found them to be helpful.

- Accept what you can't change.
- Change what you can.
- Laugh at the rest.
- Look to the future not the past.
- Look forward to something everyday.
- Lose yourself in action or you will wither in despair.
- Look for the good in others.
- Express gratitude and love.
- Keep your eyes on the scriptures and the living Prophet.

I believe that none of these points needs an explanation, with the possible exception of one: "Look forward to something everyday." For a number of years, one of my fellow teachers was Brother Ed J. Pinegar. He is a gifted teacher whose level of energy is almost childlike. I asked him one day, "Ed, how do you do it? Your level of genuine excitement and enthusiasm is amazing."

His reply caused me to add one more item to my Optimism List, and has made a positive difference in my life. He said, "I try to put at least one activity in my day that I look forward to doing."

The look on my face indicated that we weren't communicating.

He continued, "Today at 3:30 I have an appointment to play tennis. I love tennis, and it keeps me excited all day just thinking about it. If possible, I try to place the activity in the afternoon."

As I pondered his words, I realized the genius of his simple plan. From that day forward, I have attempted to schedule something in each day that feeds the enthusiastic child in me. It might be racquetball, swimming, basketball, or riding my bike, but the activity is something that feeds energy into my day just by looking forward to it. Then, when the activity is complete, my battery has been recharged enough to energetically face the rest of the evening. That is why Ed suggested placing the activity in the afternoon if at all possible.

Some who read this may question a person's ability to find optimism, and even happiness, when life's circumstances could best be described as terrible. We need look no further than a period in the Book of Mormon to find an example. During the darkest hours of war, the scriptures describe the activities in the land as quarrelings, murdering, plundering, idolatry, whoredoms, and abominations (see Alma 50:21).

It would be easy to question how anyone could be optimistic or happy during times like those. Yet the scriptures relate that "those who were faithful in keeping the commandments of the Lord were delivered at all times, . . . [And] *there never was a happier time* among the people of Nephi" (Alma 50:22–23; italics added).

What a perfect example for us: In the darkest of times, keep the commandments and look optimistically to the future. It is a helpful reminder to me.

Note

1. Dennis B. Neuenschwander, "Holy Place, Sacred Space," *Ensign*, Apr. 2003, 75.
2. Brigham Young, *Discourses of Brigham Young*, compiled by John A. Widstoe (Salt Lake City: Deseret Book, 1954), 264.
3. *Teaching of the Presidents of the Church—Joseph F. Smith* (Salt Lake City: The Church of Jesus Christ of Latter-day Saints, 1998), 299.
4. *Gospel Doctrine* (Salt Lake City, Utah: Deseret Book, 19th Printing, 1975) 316–17.
5. Phillip Roos, *The Osiris Factor* (Springville, Utah: Bonneville Books, 2002), 49.
6. Gordon B. Hinckley, "Joined Together in Love and Faith," *Ensign*, Nov. 1985, 86.
7. Gordon B. Hinckley, *New York Times* interview, 1995.
8. Gordon B. Hinckley, Interview with Larry King, Dec. 24, 2004.
9. Gordon B. Hinckley, *Standing For Something* (New York: Random House, 2000), 99–107.
10. Gordon B. Hinckley, *Way To Be* (Texas: Simon and Schuster, 2002), 81–84.

chapter five

Gratitude

When I first wrote this book, I tried to place optimism and gratitude within the same chapter because not only are these two closely related, but they just seem to flow into each other. In most instances, it would seem impossible to have gratitude without being optimistic, and when we are optimistic we are naturally grateful for so many things in life. My reason for not carrying through with placing them in the same chapter is simply due to the amount of space—it would have been a rather long chapter! However, I will invite the reader to not completely separate these two virtues.

I have consistently made the point that what we think determines the world in which we live, so as we change internally, our external world changes as well. Some time ago, I was visiting with a young man who was complaining about the place in which he lived. He concluded his negative treatise with, "Well, I guess the only solution to this problem is that I'll just have to move."

In my opinion, his negative circumstances had more to do with his attitude than his environment.

I responded with, "There is only one thing that might cause that plan to backfire."

The look on his face indicated that he wanted to know just what I was thinking. I continued, "When you move, you have to take yourself along. After a while these problems will likely show up again."

It wasn't too long into our visit that I realized that his time, as well as mine, was being wasted in this conversation. He was convinced that he was the victim of his problems, rather than being the author of them. In my mind, I determined that he would have to travel down that road a little farther before his heart might be opened to a different perspective.

Wendell J. Ashton wrote:

> I have been thinking of two women. The husband of one was an able man whose profession brought him to our city. She often was unhappy in our area. She was bothered by the mountains, the majestic, snow-crowned monarchs which so many visitors admire. She said the mountains seemed to be "closing in on me." Her attitude toward the mountains made her miserable, and others, too.
>
> Then there is a tall, blonde woman with peach-blossom complexion who taught school before she met in Washington, D.C., the man who became her husband. His work with the United States State Department took them to Mexico, then Uganda. . . .
>
> In Africa she found new people and problems. Women daily carried water on their heads to their round, thatched, mud-walled homes. Clothes and sheets which were hung out to dry must be ironed thoroughly to kill mango fly eggs before they hatched and began burrowing into human skin. (The irons were generally the kind you heated by putting hot coals into them.) Food must be periodically checked for mildew. Insect poison must be placed around the edges of cupboards, closets, and door entrances. There was the season of big, green katydids, swarming around arc lights "like a snowstorm," with natives gathering them in buckets, sheets, or bags to eat raw.
>
> But the tall, blonde woman decided she would like Uganda—and she did, immensely. She fell in love with the people. . . .
>
> As I have gone through some of her letters from Mexico and Uganda, I have found lines like these:
>
> "I felt I was the most blessed girl in the world."
>
> "I had never been happier . . . I was sure that somebody 'up there' was working overtime in my behalf." . . .
>
> Her attitude about life keeps reminding me that, as someone once said, happiness is the quality of learning to like what you must do.[1]

Notice how her expression of gratitude flowed from her mind-set of optimism. While gratitude and optimism are different by definition, they are often mirror images of each other in expression.

Attitude in the Book of Mormon

We need to look no further than the Book of Mormon for evidence of the need to maintain a positive attitude. An amazing contrast is created in the story of Lehi's family's travels from Jerusalem to Bountiful. In order to make my point, let's review the multitude of circumstances that Nephi had in common with his brothers Laman and Lemuel: (1) They were born and raised in the same home by the same parents; (2) they were raised within the same religious beliefs; (3) they married into the same family (their wives were sisters so they had the same in-laws); (4) they experienced the same harsh weather conditions in the trip to Bountiful; and (5) they ate (for the most part) the same food on the journey.

We could make further comparisons, but this is enough for me to illustrate the point. In short, their experience at a physical level was just about as similar as it could possibly be. Let us examine the contrast between the attitudes expressed by Nephi as opposed to Laman and Lemuel during their eight-year journey from Jerusalem to Bountiful.

Following the marriage of Lehi's sons to Ishmael's daughters, Nephi stated, "I, Nephi, had been blessed of the Lord exceedingly" (1 Nephi 16:8).

Contrast these positive words with the attitude expressed by Laman and Lemuel at about the same time: "Behold, these many years we have suffered in the wilderness, which time we might have enjoyed our possessions and the land of our inheritance; yea, and we might have been happy" (1 Nephi 17:21).

Nephi was happy because he made a choice to be happy. His happiness was not based on the food, weather, or the events of the day—he looked for the positive because he was positive. Laman and Lemuel chose to be unhappy because of their circumstances.

This point is further illustrated by viewing Laman and Lemuel following Nephi's return to the tent of his father, after he had been granted the same vision on the Tree of Life his father had seen. His unworthy brothers are described as "being *hard* in their hearts" in four separate verses in 1 Nephi 15 (see 1 Nephi 15:3–4,10–11; italics added.) Based on the premise that we see the world as we are, it could be predicted that Laman and Lemuel would see their world as being "hard."

True to form, following Nephi's encouragement to his brothers, they stated, "Thou hast declared unto us *hard* things" (1 Nephi 16:1; italics added). Nephi's words were seen by his brothers as hard, not because the words were hard, but because Laman and Lemuel were hard.

Nephi reinforces the truth that Laman and Lemuel attitude had created their "hard hearted" view of the world: "The guilty taketh the truth to be hard" (1 Nephi 16:2).

In keeping with this principle, the most lasting gift we can give others is who we are. This is true of all of us, even Satan. Lehi stated, "And because he had fallen from heaven, and had become *miserable* forever, he sought also the *misery* of all mankind" (2 Nephi 2:18; italics added).

It makes sense that the only gift Satan could give us is misery because he "had become miserable forever." For a number of years, my Church calling was working with the inmates at the Utah State Prison. In this setting I realized that you don't have to die to go to hell. Hell is a lifestyle before it is a place. Prior to hell being a lifestyle, it would first be an attitude, or just a way of perceiving the world. This line of reasoning would be true of heaven, as well.

Dale Carnegie wrote:

> I am deeply convinced that our peace of mind and the joy we get out of living depends not on where we are, or what we have, or who we are, but solely upon our mental attitude. Outward conditions have very little to do with it. For example, let's take the case of old John Brown, who was hanged for seizing the United States arsenal at Harpers Ferry and trying to incite the slaves to rebellion. He rode away to the gallows, sitting on his coffin. The jailer who rode beside him was nervous and worried. But old John Brown was calm and cool. Looking up at the Blue Ridge mountains of Virginia, he exclaimed, "What a beautiful country! I never had an opportunity to really see it before." . . . Yes, if we cherish creative thought of courage and calmness, we can enjoy the scenery while sitting on our coffin, riding to the gallows.[2]

The Book of Mormon gives us no indication that Laman and Lemuel ever understood this truth.

Promises to Those Who Find Gratitude

A few years ago, I stumbled across something that has had a powerful impact in my attitude toward life. I noticed that President Gordon B.

Hinckley spoke often on the topic of gratitude. What I didn't realize until I began a serious search through this Prophet's words was that he gave specific promises to those who have the gift of gratitude in contrast to warnings to those who view the world through the lens of ingratitude.

I will list a few of these quotes, placing the consequences of gratitude in *italics*, while underlining the consequences of ingratitude:

> Gratitude is a sign of *maturity*. It is an indication of sincere humility. It is a hallmark of *civility*. And most of all, it is a divine principle. I doubt there is anything in which we more offend the Almighty than in our tendency to forget His mercies and to be ungrateful for that which He has given us. . . . Where there is gratitude, there is *humility* instead of pride, *generosity* rather than selfishness. . . . we would do well, also, to cultivate within ourselves a spirit of thanksgiving for the blessing of life itself and for the marvelous gifts and privileges we enjoy. . . . Many selfish, arrogant, and usually miserable people in this world walk without gratitude.[3]

> Gratitude creates the most *wonderful feeling*. It can *resolve disputes*. It can *strengthen friendships*. And it *makes us better men and women*. The habit of saying thank you is the mark of a *cultivated mind*. . . . walk with gratitude in your hearts. Be thankful for the wonderful blessings that are yours. . . . even thank [the Lord] for your struggles, for they *will make you strong*—if you will let them. *You will find people responding to you differently than they have before*. And interestingly, you will find that you are *happier* than you have been.[4]

> Absence of gratitude is the mark of the narrow, uneducated mind. It bespeaks lack of knowledge and the ignorance of self-sufficiency. It expresses itself in ugly egotism and frequently in malicious conduct. . . . Cultivate the spirit of thanksgiving in your lives. Make it of the very nature of your lives. *It will impart an added dimension to you character that will give depth and strength*. The Lord has said, "Blessed are the meek, for they shall inherit the earth." (Matt. 5:5) I cannot escape the interpretation that meekness implies a spirit of gratitude as opposed to an attitude of self-sufficiency, as acknowledgment of a greater power beyond oneself who is the giver of every good gift, a recognition of God and an acceptance of his commandments. This is the *beginning of wisdom*.[5]

> Where there is appreciation, there is *courtesy*, there is *concern for the rights and property of others*. Without appreciation, there is arrogance and evil. . . . Gratitude is of the *very essence of worship*."[6]

These are wonderful quotes by President Hinckley, but I believe the power of his message comes when we contrast the consequences of gratitude with those of ingratitude:

Gratitude	**Ingratitude**
Maturity	Offend the Almighty
Humility	Pride
Civility	Selfishness
Divine principle	Arrogant
Generosity	Miserable
Wonderful feeling	Narrow, uneducated mind
Resolves disputes	Lack of knowledge
Strengthen friendships	Ignorance of self-sufficiency
Makes us better men and women	Ugly egotism
Cultivated mind	Malicious conduct
Makes you strong	Evil
You will find people responding to you differently	
Happier	
It will add dimension to your character that will give depth and strength	
Beginning of wisdom	
Courtesy	
Concern for the rights and property of others	
The very essence of worship	

Could there be any greater proof that our attitudes dictate our world than placing these consequences side by side? Just the promise of "You will find people responding to you differently" indicates that the world around us begins to change when we take on the attitude of gratitude. And this is just one attitude. Imagine how our world will change as we digest more and more of the mental and emotional virtues within the gospel.

The Rippling Effect of Gratitude

I was reminded that the power of gratitude extends beyond just the person expressing it when I was speaking at a fireside at the Institute of Religion at Arizona State University. This was a few years after my six-year-old son Boyd passed away from cystic fibrosis. Following my presentation a middle-aged gentleman came forward to shake my hand. He reminded me that he had been the doctor on duty when my son passed away. He referred to the last day of my son's life when they were giving him shots of morphine so that he would not suffer during his final hours. A short time before he died, one of the nurses came into his room to administer a shot. Thinking he was asleep she gave him the injection and turned to leave the room. He looked up and meekly thanked her. She called for the other nurses and doctors on the floor to meet her in the council room and they freely shed tears due to the fact that this little boy, who was nigh unto death, still had the presence of mind to say "thank you" at such a difficult moment in his life.[7]

As a father, I was grateful for his tribute to my son. As a teacher, I was reminded of the positive rippling effect that gratitude can have on everyone present. The power of gratitude is enhanced when it is honestly presented in a setting that would seem difficult to be grateful in.

Sister Chieko N. Okazaki shared this example:

> Maren Mouritsen told the women at BYU's women's conference about her mother who had suffered "a series of debilitating strokes that left her completely paralyzed on the left side, and without speech." When Maren was home for the summer after her first year at college, she and her father would get her mother ready for church, go to choir practice, and then walk back to get her before Sunday School. (They lived near the chapel.) Then one Sunday, Maren went back for her mother and discovered that she "had rolled out the front door and onto the ramp that we had built shortly after she became ill. There was the wheelchair and my mother—smack dab in the middle of the zinnias and pansies. Fearing the worst, I hurried to her side, only to find her propped up against the wall. With her only good hand she had written in the dirt, 'Flowers pretty.' "[8]

For well over a century and a half, missionaries all over the world have been reading Moroni 10:3–5 to illustrate the manner in which a revelation regarding the truthfulness of the Book of Mormon can be received.

While it is true that we may receive a witness of the Book of Mormon in this manner, verse five indicates that it also applies to revelation in general. "And by the power of the Holy Ghost ye may know the truth of all things" (Moroni 10:5).

Verse 3 gives an important prerequisite that is helpful in obtaining revelation: "Remember how merciful the Lord hath been unto the children of men, from the creation of Adam even down until the time that ye shall receive these things" (Moroni 10:3).

This "remembering the mercies of the Lord" has been identified as the attitude of gratitude. What an amazing thing to consider that gratitude for the Lord's mercies in our lives opens the door to revelation. When we are able to appreciate the Lord's tender mercies even in the face of adversity, the window of revelation is often opened to us.

God Needs Brave Sons

President Henry B. Eyring gave evidence to gratitude's connection with the Lord's tender mercies in a story he told about his father:

> To appreciate this story, you have to realize that it occurred when he was nearly eighty and had bone cancer. He had bone cancer so badly in his hips that he could hardly move. The pain was great.
>
> Dad was the senior high councilor in his stake, and he had the responsibility for the welfare farm. An assignment was given to weed a field of onions, so Dad assigned himself to go work on the farm. He never told me how hard it was, but I have met several people who were with him that day. I talked to one of them on the phone, and he said that he was weeding in the row next to Dad through much of the day. He told me the same thing that others who were there that day have told me. He said that the pain was so great that Dad was pulling himself along on his stomach with his elbows. He couldn't kneel. The pain was too great for him to kneel. Everyone who has talked to me about that day has remarked how Dad smiled and laughed and talked happily with them as they worked in that field of onions.
>
> Now, this is the joke Dad told me on himself afterward. He said he was there at the end of the day. After all the work was finished and the onions were all weeded, someone said to him, "Henry, good heavens! You didn't pull those weeds, did you? Those weeds were sprayed two days ago, and they were going to die anyway."
>
> Dad just roared. He thought that was the funniest thing. He

thought it was a great joke on himself. He had worked through the day in the wrong weeds. They had been sprayed and would have died anyway.

When Dad told me this story, I knew how tough it was. So I asked him, "Dad, how could you make a joke out of that? How could you take it so pleasantly?" . . . He said, "Hal, I wasn't there for the weeds." . . .

One night when I was not with him and the pain seemed more than he could bear, he somehow got out of bed and on his knees beside it—I know not how. He pled with God to know why he was suffering so. And the next morning he said, with quiet firmness, "I know why now. God needs brave sons."[9]

President Eyring's father's consistent attitude, even in the midst of severe adversity, opened the door for revelation for him. When we can partake of the bitter cup without becoming bitter, the Lord can work with us in quietly wonderful ways. For those refined souls who can substitute bitterness with gratitude, the possibilities are that "ye may know the truth of all things" (Moroni 10:5).

Grateful for Toothbrushes

We have been invited to make gratitude a way of life, in the sense that we look for the good and then express it, even in simple things. Marjorie Pay Hinckley, wife of President Gordon B. Hinckley, challenged young adults on this subject:

I went to high school during the days of the famous Depression. It was a miserable experience. . . . Somehow it helped me to appreciate much more the prosperity we now enjoy. I know some of you think you are on a tight budget, and you are. I am glad if you are. But it is a tight budget because you have nothing else to compare with it. It isn't your fault that somehow or other you have always been able to get a new pair of shoes, whether you needed them or not. It isn't your fault that you have at least five or six changes of clothing in your crowded closet. But all of this makes it doubly hard for you to be truly grateful.

Has the fear of not being able to get an education ever struck terror into your heart: Probably not, for you knew that somehow or other you would get here and that somehow or other you will stay as long as you so desire, for this is America, where only your own indolence can keep you from the good things of life. And when you finally develop a little gratitude in your heart, make up your mind to express it. "Appreciation

> unexpressed is not appreciation." If you can't find someone to say thank you to for something, just take a look at your toothbrush and say, "Thank you for being. You are a wonderful gadget."
>
> "Thank you" is a wonderful phrase. Use it. It will add stature to your soul. Never let a day go by without saying thank you to someone for something—and especially to your Heavenly Father.[10]

As I stated earlier, I am currently involved in the recovery from my third heart attack. In fact, as I am writing this sentence it has only been a few weeks since the event. I truly hope the old saying, "The third time is the charm," is true. I have found that there have been moments lately when even being grateful for a toothbrush has been a bit of a challenge. But these words of the Lord have been helpful: "Thou shalt thank the Lord thy God in all things" (D&C 59:7). This means that we are encouraged to thank the Lord for the challenging, even painful gifts we would have never given ourselves.

I have discovered on those occasions when my attitude is contrite, the Spirit whispers to me that some of the Lord's greatest gifts are hidden in my pain. On these occasions I can see that when my body has been weakened, the Lord has my attention just long enough to strengthen my spirit. In those spiritually strengthening moments, I can honestly be grateful for my physical challenges, and I seem to be given the compensating gifts of patience and compassion. At those times my gratitude flows into optimism in such a way that it seems that my gratitude is simply a way of expressing optimism.

Some people may question how gratitude can flow through a series of heart attacks. I would answer this by pointing out that when our health is threatened, we are sometimes forced to reach further than just what we see and touch. When I was young, the reflection in the mirror seemed to be the reflection of my worth. I worked so hard at maintaining the best reflection I possibly could. The value system of youth is intertwined with the appearance and performance of the body. However, through the process of aging our bodies begin to let us down, and we are forced to look deeper than just our reflection. Nowadays, placing the same price tag on the reflection in the mirror as I did when I was young might leave me feeling a bit devalued.

For me, these days, the standard which was once connected to looking good has been replaced with the desire of being good. The youthful mentality of "good is as good looks" has matured into "good is as good does." In this mind-set, the scriptures and the words of Latter-day prophets have taken on a greater significance. It is at these moments that my spiritual stride is lengthened and the fear of having a heart attack or any other earthly challenge is the furthest thing from my mind. This perspective allows me to have gratitude for things I would have never appreciated at a more youthful stage in my life. Blessed is the young person who can gain this understanding without having to go through the time and energies of aging.

My daughter Aubrey, who lives with her family in Lund, Nevada, called me recently to share a story read by one her primary students. It captures the truth that our appreciation for the world around us has more to do with us than it does the world:

> One day a father of a very wealthy family took his son on a trip to the country with the firm purpose of showing his son how poor people live. They spent a couple of days and nights on the farm of what would be considered a very poor family.
>
> On their return from their trip, the father asked his son, "How was the trip?"
>
> "It was great, Dad."
>
> "Did you see how poor people live?"
>
> "Oh yeah," said the son.
>
> "So, tell me, what did you learn from the trip?" asked the father.
>
> The son answered: "I saw that we have one dog and they had four. We have a pool that reaches to the middle of our garden and they have a creek that has no end. We have imported lanterns in our garden and they have the stars at night. Our patio reaches to the front yard and they have the whole horizon. We have a small piece of land to live on and they have fields that go beyond our sight. We have servants who serve us, but they serve others. We buy our food, but they grow theirs. We have walls around our property to protect us, they have friends to protect them."
>
> The boy's father was speechless.
>
> Then his son added, "Thanks Dad, for showing me how poor we are."
>
> Isn't perspective a wonderful thing? Makes you wonder what would happen if we all gave thanks for everything we have, instead of worrying about what we don't have.[11]

Three Word Analogy

This point is easily brought home by using a variation of the "three word" mental exercise that I shared in chapter two. In this teaching tool, I divide the people in the audience in two groups. The first group (group A) is asked to put their heads down, while the second group (group B) is invited to silently view the large screen behind me. Group B is shown these three words: Apples, Oranges, and Fruit.

I then ask group B to put their heads down and quietly think of the three words they have just seen. Group A is asked to lift up their eyes to silently view another set of words: Violence, Lust, and Sex.

Now, I ask both groups to have their heads down and simply ponder the three words which I have been presented to them. With their heads still down, I tell them that I am now placing a four letter word on the screen in front of them, but I have left a letter out of the word. I remind them that in a moment they will be invited to look at the screen, and instantly their minds will fill in the missing letter. I then project R_PE on the screen behind me.

Next, I ask them all to view the screen without sharing with each other the word that their minds have instantly completed. Turning to group B, I ask them the word they saw on the board. Nearly 100 percent of them will say RIPE. Many will be surprised that this unanimity has occurred with no consultation with others in the group. Their singleness of thought obviously has occurred due to the fact that they have focused their minds on the same three words.

Now, I turn to group A, and ask them to share the word that they saw. It is not unusual (especially for an adult group) for the group to hesitate. To which, I quickly respond, "How many of you initially saw the word RAPE?" This causes some nervous laughter, as each individual understands that he or she wasn't the only one to see this word.

I then place the following on the screen:

Group A	Group B
Violence	Apples
Lust	Oranges
Sex	Fruit

I remind the group that our view of the world is a projection of our own thoughts, reinforced over and over again. If three words viewed independently on a screen can alter the way we see R_PE, is it any wonder the view of the world (for so many) has taken on such a dark perspective? With all that is happening in television, movies, and music, it is not difficult to see why the mind-set of so many has taken a turn for the worse.

Therefore, our ability to feel and express gratitude has much more to do with what is happening within us than what is happening in the world around us. As we change our internal perspective, our world changes. As we digest the positive lean of optimism in our entertainment, our friends, and all that we consume, it is only natural that gratitude for life and its gifts will follow. Gratitude is a mind-set long before it springs forth as an expression. It is a heart filled with gratitude, which sets the stage for the lengthening of our stride.

Notes

1. Wendell J. Ashton, *To Thine Own Self* (Salt Lake City: Bookcraft, 1972), 59-61)
2. Carnegie, *How to Stop Worrying and Start Living,* 95–96.
3. Hinckley, *Standing For Something,* 90–91.
4. Hinckley, *Way To Be,* 15–20.
5. Gordon B. Hinckley, *From My Generation To Yours. . . With Love!* (Salt Lake City: Deseret Book, 1973), 11, 13.
6. Hinckley, *Teachings of Gordon B. Hinckley,* 247, 250.
7. See K. D. Bassett, *The Barber's Song* (Springville, Utah: Cedar Fort, 2005), 91.
8. Chieko N. Okazaki, *Cat's Cradle* (Salt Lake City, Utah: Bookcraft, 1993), 128)
9. Henry B. Eyring, *To Draw Closer To God* (Salt Lake City, Utah: Bookcraft, 1997), 101–102, 116.
10. *Glimpses Into The Life and Heart of Marjorie Pay Hinckley,* ed. by Virginia H. Pearce (Salt Lake City, Utah: Deseret Book, 1999), 90–91.
11. Anonymous author

chapter six

Finding Peace in a World of Conflict

Up until now I have focused on our mental and emotional capacity to rise above life's challenges. However, in the world we live in, which is filled with so much war and economic strain, the only real hope is to be found in the doctrines of Christ. This chapter will focus on the peace which comes from knowing those truths that run deeper than what we read in today's newspaper.

I had an experience on September 11, 2001 that contrasted the tragic events of the day. That morning began like any other, until my wife spoke these words to me as I was exiting the shower: "Some nut just flew a plane into one of the twin towers in New York City." Then, with a quick breakfast, and a kiss and hug, I was off to work. Now, this was during the time that I was driving the Rustmobile to work. (Remember, it did not have a radio.) Therefore, as I was moving down the freeway toward my first class, I was totally unaware of the second plane that hit the towers or the heroic efforts of the passengers on the third plane in thwarting the terrorists. In fact, I was uninformed regarding any connection to terrorism at all.

Arriving just in time to teach my class, I did not speak to any of my fellow teachers or students in the hallway regarding the events of the morning. However, as I entered the classroom there was an odd feeling that reflected in the faces of my students. This was a returned missionary Book of Mormon class, which was normally filled with laughter and light conversation before we got started. On this day, they looked stunned, like they were sitting at a funeral waiting for some kind of comfort.

After shaking hands with each of my students, we began the class by singing a hymn. Again, something was different. Normally, they sang like missionaries at a zone conference, full of enthusiasm and spirit. Today, their singing was reverent—almost subdued.

The young man offering the opening prayer was standing behind the teacher's stand in front of the class, an arm's length away from me. His prayer was unusually long and filled with great sincerity. During the prayer, something happened that I have never experienced before in my thirty years of teaching. I felt prompted to open my eyes and turn over the paper that I had written my lesson on, which was sitting on the teacher's stand. I started writing scriptures just as fast as they came to my mind. Also, I referenced page numbers to quotes by the Brethren from the commentary we used in class as quickly as I could put them on paper. Without hesitation, I continued to write even for a few moments after the student had offer the prayer. I'm sure the class was a little surprised as they looked up from their bowed heads to see what I was doing. While I was totally unaware of the direction I would be taking this information, I was completely confident that this was something which I should be doing. The class waited patiently for me to finish. I found it odd that no one spoke after the prayer or openly questioned my scribbling. Even the young man praying seemed unaffected by my behavior, which at best could be described as rude. Surely he had noticed that I had been writing during his prayer, right?

Then, without any introduction or explanation, I took the students through the scriptures and quotes by the Brethren that I had referenced during the prayer. While I knew these scriptures and the quotes, I was totally clueless to their context in the tragic activities of the morning. I found it odd that there were no questions or comments by my students. Even so, I was aware that the Spirit present on that occasion was edifying to them. I found myself teaching with a power and sensibility that went far beyond my normal capabilities.

I could not understand the show of emotion by some of the students during class and was even more taken back by their embraces and sincere expressions of gratitude immediately following the class period. In all of this, not one of my students referred to the actions of the terrorists.

As soon as I stepped into the hallway, one of my fellow teachers stopped me and said, "Have you heard the latest?" He then filled me in regarding the events of the morning. I proceeded to my office and reread every scripture and quote I had just shared with the students. I felt like my experience in the class had been like the Lamanites whom the Lord said "were baptized with fire and with the Holy Ghost, and they knew it not" (3 Nephi 9:20). While I had certainly been aware of the Spirit in the class, I definitely "knew it not" concerning the reasoning behind the lesson I was presenting.

I joined my tears with the ones I had witnessed in class, understanding that the Lord had shown his "tender mercies" (see 1 Nephi 1:20) to my students. He inspired one who was unprepared to deal with the tragic events of the morning and allowed me to be a vehicle for the Spirit. This not only blessed my students but my life as well. I was overwhelmed with the thought that in all the morning's turmoil, the Lord would be mindful of these precious young people who had served Him so faithfully on their missions.

The words of Elder Jeffrey R. Holland to this age group are appropriate:

> God is in charge. He knows your name and He knows your need. . . . So, in a world of tribulation—and there will always be plenty of it—let's remember our faith. . . . God is watching over His world, His Church, His leaders, and He is certainly watching over you. . . . Is there a happy future for you and your posterity in these latter days? Absolutely! . . . Will there be difficult times when those ominous latter-day warnings and prophecies are fulfilled? Of course there will. . . . God not only lives, He loves us. He loves you. Everything he does is for our good and our protection. . . . He will shelter us from the storm. . . . I leave an apostolic blessing on each one of you individually within the sound of my voice that you will live with confidence, optimism, faith, and devotion. . . . I bless you to feel the joy of the Saints in the latter days—never crippling anxiety or destructive despair."[1]

In the days following the tragedy of the Twin Towers, I found the words of Elder Orson Pratt, spoken nearly 132 years earlier, to be relevant. While I believe Elder Pratt was speaking of a time that included a much wider range of destruction, I found a portion of his words to have an eerie similarity to those of the workers involved in the frantic search for survivors: "The great, powerful and populous city of New York, . . . will in a few years become a mass of ruins. The people will wonder while gazing on the ruins that cost hundreds of millions to build, *what has become of its inhabitants.*"[2] Those of us who watched the continuous news coverage of this tragedy will remember the impossible task that stretched out for months and months to find bodies and identify the names of the victims.

The events of 9/11 occurred on Tuesday. On Friday of that same week, Elder F. David Stanley of the Seventy visited the Orem Institute of Religion. He met first with the faculty, and then addressed the students at our weekly devotional. He told us that earlier he had visited briefly with President Hinckley regarding that day's assignment to speak to our students. These are the specific words he shared with us: "President Hinckley told me to tell you that the protective hand of the Lord is still over America." As he said those words, I felt the same comforting sense of peace that I did following my Book of Mormon class on Tuesday.

He told us that shortly after the terrorist tragedy on Tuesday, President Bush personally called President Hinckley to come to the White House to visit with him. The Prophet met with him on Thursday. Each Thursday since the building of the Salt Lake Temple, the living Prophet has always met with the Brethren in the temple. This was one of the rare times in our Church's history that the Prophet was not in the temple at the weekly meeting with the Apostles. Instead, he was at the White House meeting with the President of the United States regarding the events of 9/11.

We were told how President Bush was presented a Book of Mormon from President Hinckley with these words emphasized: "Behold, this is a choice land and whatsoever nation shall possess it shall be free from bondage, and from captivity, and from all other nations under heaven, if they will but serve the God of the land, who is Jesus Christ" (Ether 2:12).

I was aware that a number of years earlier, President Hinckley had read the same scripture to Ronald Reagan.[3]

It is important to make note of the conditional nature of the promise given in the Book of Ether. President Hinckley did so on another occasion: "We can so live that we can call upon the Lord for His protection and guidance. . . . We cannot expect His help if we are unwilling to keep His commandments. We in this Church have evidence enough of the penalties of disobedience in the examples of both the Jaredite and the Nephite nations. Each went from glory to utter destruction because of wickedness."[4]

And today, as we follow the living prophet President Thomas S. Monson, I feel the same sense of peace in a world of conflict. It brings to mind the initial chapter of what is called the "war chapters" in the Book of Mormon. Before Moroni went to battle he "sent certain men unto . . . [the prophet Alma], desiring him that he should inquire of the Lord" (Alma 43:23).

With all of Moroni's knowledge in military matters—with all his preparations for battle—he did not move forward without the direction of the prophet. Following the living prophet in times of trial is as relevant today as it was in ancient times.

In economic times like these—times filled with so much turmoil—I feel the hearts of many of the young people I serve are trembling with fear. The Book of Mormon and the latter-day prophets give us an assurance of hope. Nephi saw the events in this land that lead to our times. Then he wrote something that reads like the headline in today's newspaper (it must first be noted that Nephi referred to the people who would settle this land as Gentiles, because of the nations from which we have our roots): "I beheld that the power of God was with them, . . . And I, Nephi, beheld that the Gentiles that had gone out of captivity were *delivered out of the hands of all other nations*" (1 Nephi 13:18–19, italics added).

This prophecy is reinforced in our day when we read the Lord's words through the Prophet Jacob: "Said God, . . . the Gentiles shall be blessed upon the land. And this land shall be a land of liberty unto the Gentiles, . . . *And I will fortify this land against all other nations*" (2 Nephi 10:10–12, italics added).

In both of these scriptures the Lord promises protection against "all other nations." The scriptures don't say "most other nations," but "all other nations." Could the ancient prophets have said anything more reassuring to the Saints in this land than this?

No less comforting are the words of our latter-day leaders. The Prophet Harold B. Lee wrote: "Men may fail in this country, earthquakes may come, seas may heave beyond their bounds, there may be great drought, disaster, and hardship, but this nation, founded on principles laid down by men whom God raised up, *will never fail*. . . . Yes, I repeat, men may fail, but this nation won't fail. . . . I plead with you not to preach pessimism. . . . It is the nation that will stand despite whatever trials or crises it may yet have to pass through."[5]

President Ezra Taft Benson gave these reassuring words as another witness: "But whatever may be our fate, be assured that this [Constitution] will stand. We . . . face difficult days in this beloved land. . . . It may cost us blood before we are through. It is my conviction, however, that *when the Lord comes, the Stars and Stripes will be floating on the breeze over this people.*"[6]

With the threat of military destruction that hangs like a cloud over all the peoples of the earth, the words of the Lord remind us: "Do I not hold the destinies of all the armies of the nation of the earth?" (D&C 117:6).

In response to the words of Presidents Lee and Benson, the question could be raised, "Why won't this country fail?" It would be disappointing to think there may be some members of the Church in this land who would say we will remain free because we are more righteous than people in other countries. Those who have traveled to other countries and spent time with those citizens recognize that this assumption is untrue.

The Lord gives evidence to why this nation will remain free: "For it is wisdom in the Father that they should be established in this land, and be set up as a free people by the power of the Father that these things [the restored Gospel and the Book of Mormon] might come forth" (3 Nephi 21:4).

Elder Mark E. Peterson called this thinking "the destiny of America. . . . Old Glory was raised up because there was to be a restoration of the gospel."[7]

It would not be hard to predict what would happen to our ability to send missionaries throughout the world, as well as build temples and chapels outside the United States, if this country was not free.

President Benson stated why this nation must remain free: "This then becomes the Lord's base of operations in these latter days. And this base will not be shifted out of its place—the land of America."[8]

Lehi referred to this land as "a land which is choice above all other lands" (2 Nephi 1:5). Some may think that the word *choice* means that the people, or the mountains, valleys, rivers, and streams are somehow better than those found in other lands. This assumption would be a mistake. The word *choice* has to do with our ability to make choices. It has to do with the opportunity in this land to exercise the agency, which is the result of being a free people. As the Lord said, "To be set up as a free people by the power of the Father" (3 Nephi 21:4).

Even If by Fire

There may be those (even in the Church) who question how the Lord is able to fulfill this promise and at the same time allow the gift of agency to all people. The answer to this is given to us by Nephi in the Book of Mormon: "Wherefore, he will preserve the righteous by his power, even if it so be that the fullness of his wrath must come, and the righteous be preserved, even unto the destruction of their enemies by fire. Wherefore, the righteous need not fear; for thus saith the prophet, they shall be saved, even if it so be as by fire" (1 Nephi 22:17).

President Benson used this same verse of scripture to remind us that America will remain free: "Yes, it was here under a free government and a strong nation that protection was provided for His restored Church. Now *God will not permit his base of operations—America—to be destroyed.* He has promised protection to this land if we will but serve the God of the land. He has also promised protection to the righteous even if necessary, to send fire from heaven to destroy their enemies (1 Nephi 22:17). No, God's base of operations will not be destroyed."[9]

This scripture, as well as the words of President Benson, illustrate the fact that the Lord has the ability to protect His people. This particular scripture is a duel prophecy in that it speaks to more than one time period. The "fire" mentioned numerous times in this verse of scripture obviously refers to the Second Coming, but it also refers to our day. The reader may question this assumption by declaring that "I haven't seen any fire from heaven in my life."

In support of Nephi's promise of protection by fire, he stated, "he will not suffer that the wicked shall destroy the righteous. . . . the righteous shall not perish; . . . the righteous need not fear." (1 Nephi 22:16, 19–20, 22).

Elder Dallin H. Oaks bore his witness regarding this promise: "I am grateful for the Book of Mormon promise to us of the last days that 'the righteous need not fear,' for the Lord 'will preserve the righteous by his power' (1 Nephi 22:17)."[10]

The scriptures, as well as the latter-day prophets, give us evidence to three ways the Lord protects His people "even if it so be as by fire."

The Holy Ghost

The Holy Ghost is often referred to as fire (see Helaman 5:44–45) and one of the functions of the Holy Ghost is to protect those thus endowed with this gift. The Apostle Robert D. Hales stated in a general conference: "Through the still, small voice of His Spirit, the Lord will protect us, help us, and guide us."[11]

The Prophet Wilford Woodruff gave evidence of the protection offered through the Holy Ghost:

> I was sent to Boston by President Brigham Young. . . . While on the road there, I drove my carriage one evening into the yard of Brother Williams. . . . I had my wife and children in the carriage. After I turned out my team and had my supper I went to bed in the carriage. I had not been there but a few minutes when the Spirit said to me, "Get up and move that carriage." I told my wife I had to get up and move the carriage. She said, "What for?" I said, "I don't know." That is all she asked me on such occasions; when I told her I did not know, that was enough. I got up and moved my carriage . . . I then looked around me and went to bed. The same Spirit said, 'Go and move your animals from that oak tree.' They were two hundred yards from where my carriage was. I went and moved my horses, and put them in a little hickory grove. I again went to bed.
>
> In thirty minutes a whirlwind came up and broke that oak tree off . . . and fell . . . right where [my wagon] had stood. What would have been the consequences if I had not listened to that Spirit? . . . that was the still, small voice to me—no earthquake, no thunder, no lightning—but the still, small voice of the Spirit of God. It saved my life.[12]

The Book of Mormon declares that all people, "reap eternal happiness or eternal misery, according to the spirit which they listeth to obey, whether it be a good spirit or a bad one. For every man receiveth wages of him whom he listeth to obey" (Alma 3:26). The protection promised by obeying this "good spirit" is one of those "wages."

Angels

The Prophet Brigham Young said, "God has been and is our helper, and is on our right and left, and round about us like a wall of fire to defend this people, if they serve him with an undivided heart."[13] Along with the Holy Ghost as protection, the righteous have been given the promise of further help from the other side of the veil.

Brigham Young identified this "wall of fire" that defends God's people: "When the Lord commands those invisible beings, . . . yes, millions and millions more than the inhabitants of this earth, they can fight your battles."[14]

Parley P. Pratt bore witness to this angelic protection from the other side of the veil: "I have lain months in gloomy dungeons, and been loaded with chains. I have been visited there by visions of Angels and Spirits, and been delivered by miracles."[15]

Closer to our day, Gordon B. Hinckley testified, "You have the power of heavenly beings to guide you, to protect you, to bless you."[16]

Elder Jeffrey R. Holland said:

> I testify that angels are still sent to help us, . . . ministrations will be to the righteous until the end of time. I ask everyone within the sound of my voice to . . . remember the Lord has said He 'would fight (our) battles, (our) children's battles, and (the battles of our) children's children.' (D&C 98:37) . . . May we all believe more readily in, and have more gratitude for, the Lord's promise as contained in one of President Monson's favorite scriptures: "I will go before your face. I will be on your right hand and on your left, . . . my Spirit shall be in your (heart), and mine angels round about you, to bear you up." (D&C 84:88)[17]

Would it be too much to assume that as a part of that promised protection of angels that each one of us has a large group who are encouraging us from the other side of the veil? Elder Paul H. Dunn wrote:

> Each one of us has a cheering section . . . We sometimes doubt it, but it is true nevertheless. . . . Of that I am sure! Even when you feel all alone, there are those who are rooting for you. . . . All of us have parents, friends, or other loved ones who have passed away. . . . Do parents stop caring because they die? Are friends no longer friends at death? Does caring stop at the grave? . . . And what of those yet unborn? Do they have interest in your success? Your unborn children watch you from above with great interest and concern. . . . Probably millions of spirits yet to be born cheer loudly for the millions of us who prepare the way for them. . . . Every person in this life has a cheering section. It is composed of those around us, those who have passed over to the other side, and those who are yet to come.[18]

The Priesthood

Brigham Young bore witness of the protecting hand of the angels, as well as the Holy Ghost, but he added a third element as a part of the protective wages from our Heavenly Father: "He is here ready by his agents, the angels, and by the power of his Holy Spirit and Priesthood . . . to bring most perfect and absolute deliverance unto all who put their trust in him."[19]

President Wilford Woodruff adds further light to the protection under the priesthood: "The priesthood of God who honor their priesthood, and who are worthy of their blessings are the only ones who shall have this safety and protection. . . . If you do your duty, and I do my duty, we'll have protection, and shall pass through the afflictions in peace and in safety."[20]

A student of mine named Jacob Jorgensen shared this journal entry with me regarding the power of the Priesthood during his experience as a soldier in Iraq:

> While preparing to go to Iraq I received a blessing from my Father. I was promised that I would be watched over and protected. I felt the love of my Heavenly Father and trusted in the words that were said in the blessing.
>
> After four months in Iraq, I was given an impression regarding the protecting hand of the Lord promised in my Father's blessing. This feeling did not leave me over the next few weeks. I continued to strive every day to live worthy, although I was never perfect, and the times that I was slow to repent were the only fearsome and scary moments I had in Iraq.
>
> During that time we had been fighting an insurgent who was the best "Roadside Bomber" we had ever encountered. Our job was to clear the roadside bombs up and down all the streets. I was driving the command vehicle, which was the fourth vehicle in line. The plan was for the lead vehicle to go to the end of the street and clear all the bombs while the rest of us stayed back.
>
> As we approached my mind was caught away from the events of the moment and I saw a 5-ton truck (which holds up to two squads of marines or about 26 soldiers) blow up, killing everyone inside. After the vision closed, I knew I couldn't let these Marines be killed so I closed my eyes and prayed to the Lord. Remembering my Father's blessing I said, "Heavenly Father, let the roadside bomb go off on my truck. I believe we have the best chance of survival. Please let the bomb go off on my vehicle and not the Marines. These things I pray for in the name of Jesus Christ, amen." As my vehicle approached the end of the street a bomb went off under us. The blast was so big that it picked us up, almost flipping us over. The steering column broke loose from the blast and slammed against my chest. I couldn't see anything from the smoke and dust, and I could barely gasp any air because my chest had been hammered. My head was spinning from bouncing off the ceiling. My ears were ringing terribly and I could barely hear the medic yelling

in my ear asking if I was ok. I said I was good with the little air I could get, and he left to check on the others.

Just then everything went silent and a wonderful peace came over me. I had never felt so peaceful or safe in my life. The pain in my chest and head vanished—the ringing in my ears ceased. It was as if I had passed into another realm where there was nothing to distract. Then a voice that was indescribable spoke to me. It was as still and calm as a whisper, yet I heard it perfectly. It penetrated me to the core. The words he spoke to me were, "This is an answer to you prayer."

I knew there was no one to my left where the sound came from. I was aware that even if there were there was no way I could have heard him. Yet, when I turned to look I can't fully describe the feeling of peace that I felt.

Then, as quick as this spiritual experience came I was once again back to the present, with the vehicle filled with smoke and dust, accompanied by the sound of people yelling and the chaos of war around me. Yet, the peace of mind and soul that can only be understood by those who have had similar experiences, stayed with me. After gathering up my possessions and making sure all was well, I jumped out of our vehicle as happy and cheerful as a child at Christmas.

About 5 or 6 hours after it happened I returned to the base and called my mother. I didn't mention anything about it until she asked me if something had happened that day. I told her what had happened and she asked me when it had occurred. When I told her, she was quiet for a moment and related she had an impression at the exact same time. As she was driving on the freeway she was suddenly prompted by the Spirit. A feeling she had had only once before, when my brother passed away suddenly 12 years earlier. She had asked the Lord if I was gone, as well. The Spirit spoke to her and said, "Your prayers have been answered this day, he has been saved."

Later, I visited the maintenance crew who said I was the luckiest person they had ever met. They told me that it was a miracle that I was alive and still had both my legs due to the fact that the bomb had gone off directly under where I was sitting. I cannot fully express the love I feel toward the Lord. I know it was His hand that protected me. There was no scientific reason for what had happened and everyone who witnessed the event said that I was either unnaturally lucky or it was a miracle.

As time went on I was involved in many more fights, yet I never feared, wondered, or doubted that the Lord was watching over me—I

> was in his hands always. I am completely confident the only reason I was kept safe and protected was because of the Priesthood blessing given by my father.

It is through the Holy Ghost, angels, and His priesthood that the Lord fulfills his promise to our times that "they shall be saved, even if it so be as by fire" (1 Nephi 22:17).

I can personally bear witness to this promise. As a young man of about fifteen years, I was traveling in the back of a pick-up truck to a church softball game. Accompanying me were a few others who would play in the game. We were surrounded by bats, balls, and various other equipment to be used later in the day. On this warm summer afternoon, we were traveling on the old highway which goes through Live Oak, California. On an open stretch of road just outside this small town, my cousin (who was driving) pulled out to pass another car. He lost control and the truck flipped, throwing all of us like missiles out of the back of the vehicle.

The farmer working nearby told us later that he did not want to approach the scene because he was sure everyone in the back of the truck had been killed. He related to us how upon hearing the sound of screeching tires, he turned just in time to see all of us thrown through the air as the truck flipped upside down into the field across the road. To his surprise, as well as our own, we did not incur any injuries beyond some bumps, bruises, and a little soreness the following day. This would seem impossible when you consider the speed at which we were traveling (at least sixty miles per hour) and all the equipment flying out of the truck with us. Our safety was further compromised when it is understood that we landed near railroad tracks where the ground was dangerously hard, bumpy, and very uneven.

But this does not begin to tell the story from a spiritual perspective. As a young man, I did not view the world with any kind of spiritual perspective, so I did not share what actually happened with anyone for many years. Frankly, I just did not understand it until I began to have insight into the promises of protection I have just been sharing with the reader.

Just before my cousin lost control of the vehicle, everything which transpired in the next few seconds took place (for me) in slow motion. I moved to the back of the truck and braced myself against the tailgate. When the pick-up flipped, I was as in as much control as if I were jumping from a swing in the playground. It felt as if I was even able to control myself in the air to the point that I could get my feet under me to land as safely as possible. Even though I was traveling (along with everyone else) at least fifty miles per hour through the air, it was to me in slow motion. The speed of the events around me did not get back to normal until I was standing safely on the ground.

Elder Jeffrey R. Holland wrote: "If our eyes could be opened, we would see horses and chariots of fire as far as the eye can see, riding at great speed to come to our protection. [2 Kings 6:14-17.] . . . We have been given this promise from heaven."[21]

I can testify with absolute certainty that the unseen elements identified as "fire" were present on that day so many years ago. And I believe if our eyes could be opened, each one of us could be witnesses to the many times our lives have been protected throughout our earthly sojourn.

I Won't Die Before My Time

As I have shared this promise of protection in numerous settings over the years, the question is often raised, "What about the good people who die before their time?"

We have all witnessed many people who seem to leave us in a season that would seem way too soon. Elder Neal A. Maxwell wrote: "We . . . know that the days and years of righteous individuals will not be numbered less."[22]

President Ezra Taft Benson said, "It has been said that the death of a righteous man is never untimely because our Father sets the time. I believe that with all my soul."[23]

At the funeral for the Apostle Richard L. Evans, President Joseph F. Smith said, "No righteous man is ever taken before his time. In the case of faithful saints, they are simply transferred to other fields of labor. The Lord's work goes on in this life, in the world of spirits, and in the kingdoms of glory where men go after their resurrection."

We need only ask ourselves, did Jesus Christ and Joseph Smith die young? Obviously, they did. But did they die before their time? Obviously not. Was not Joseph promised that his days would not be numbered less (see D&C 122:9)?

When I heard that a dear friend of mine had lost his wife in an accident, I immediately rushed to his home. His mourning for her was coupled with the feelings that somehow, someway, he could have prevented it. I have never seen a man hurt so severely for the loss of one loved so dear. Many people had tried to console him to no avail. The first few minutes of our visit, I felt just as helpless as everyone else. As I spoke with him, I prayed that I could be inspired to say something that might ease his burden. Following about a half hour of complete frustration, I had a thought. I asked him if his wife was a righteous person. He looked at me as if I were crazy and replied, "You know she was."

I then left him with the promise that I would bring him something that would lift his burden. I went to work the next day and pulled from my files a handout with the three quotes regarding the death of righteous individuals I have just shared, along with three more pages of quotes by the Brethren reinforcing the same doctrine.

He had a strong testimony concerning the restored Gospel, so these words from those in authority empowered him in a way that was almost instantaneous. From that point on, those who came with the idea of comforting him were left with an encouragement that increased their faith.

This doctrine does not take away agency, it just empowers the faithful with the realization that God is a personal God and "He knows your name and He knows your need."[24]

Let us not be so sophisticated that we fail to recognize the promise of protection from those from the other side of the veil.

To carry on in faith, we must believe that for righteous individuals, the Lord is in the living and the dying. The Book of Mormon speaks to this. In the very first chapter, Nephi states, "I, Nephi will show unto you that the tender mercies of the Lord are over all those whom he hath chosen, because of their faith, *to make them mighty even unto the power of deliverance*" (1 Nephi 1:20, italics added).

This being made "mighty even unto the power of deliverance" is a dominant theme throughout the Book of Mormon. When Alma led the Nephites against the Amlicites, we are told that the Lord did "strengthen" the Nephites four different times in three verses (see Alma 2:18, 28, 31) to the preservation of their lives. Yet the very next chapter relates how the Nephites buried so many of their dead that "the number of the slain were not numbered, because of the greatness of their number" (Alma 3:1). We are left with the conclusion that while the Lord did "strengthen" them "to make them mighty even unto the power of deliverance," He also allowed many of these same Nephites to lose their lives. Based on the premise that "no righteous man is taken before his time," we can only assume their time had come.

Elder Dallin H. Oaks said, "Stories such as these do not mean that the servants of God are delivered from all hardship or that they are always saved from death. Some believers lose their lives in persecutions, and some suffer great hardships as a result of their faith. But the protection promised to the faithful servants of God is a reality today as it was in Bible times."[25]

We can read the wonderful account of how the stripling warriors led by Helaman were continually spared because of their obedience (see Alma 56–58). On the other hand, we are told how many of the obedient Anti-Nephi-Lehies (including fathers and grandfathers of these stripling warriors) were slain at the hands of the Lamanites (see Alma 24:21–22). Based on the sacrifices of the Anti-Nephi-Lehies, we can't assume that these youthful warriors weren't any more righteous than their parents. In fact, we are told that those Anti-Nephi-Lehies who lost their lives "were righteous people, . . . there was not a wicked man slain among them" (Alma 24:26–27).

Abinadi stated to the priests of King Noah that "God will not suffer that I shall be destroyed at this time" (Mosiah 12:13). The fact that Abinadi was executed three days later does not take away from the fact that his life had been preserved until he finished his mission.

The Book of Mormon continually reminds us that while the Lord protects the righteous to fulfill His divine purposes, He is also mindful of their mortal timetables. To be sure, the Lord is in the living as well as the dying for these individuals in the Book of Mormon.

Place of Peace

Many years ago we moved into our home in Mona. Over the years of family life, it is amazing how stuff can accumulate. We were reminded of this as we transported quite a few truckloads to our new home. With the overwhelming task of placing everything in the right rooms, our family, along with the assistance of friends and new neighbors, worked for a few days to complete the task.

My younger children would work for a little while, and then suddenly disappear within their new surroundings, anxious to be engaged in the next adventure in their lives. As I was walking into the bathroom to add to the stack of boxes already existing in the corner, I noticed a piece of paper taped to the door of the furnace room. Not thinking much about it, I traveled past the door with my mind focused on what I perceived as greater things.

A little while later, my ten-year-old son Jacob enthusiastically asked me to follow him—there was something he desperately wanted to show me. He took me by the hand to the furnace room. Proudly, he introduced me to the piece of paper on the door, which read, "Place of Peace." He then opened the door to show me his new world. As I gazed into the room I saw the water heater, as well as the furnace. I also noticed he had jammed a small desk into the corner and had filled the room with pillows, blankets, and other curious items that could easily catch on fire if they came in contact with the pilot light.

Without the slightest effort at discerning his needs and channeling his enthusiasm to a new location, I dashed his wonderful achievement by informing him in an impatient tone that this was not a play room due to its flammable nature. I concluded my discourse by letting him know that if he wanted to do something useful he could join us in the work. I delivered this message in a tone that left no doubt as to my wishes. I then went back to work.

An hour or so later I took another box into the bathroom. As I passed by the furnace room I glanced over at the paper that Jacob had taped to the door. The message "Place of Peace" had been crossed out with a giant X. Underneath it was written a new message: "There is no place of peace." Staring at these words written from the tender heart of my son, it was as if my spirit had been punched in the stomach. I was brought to the full realization of what I had done. Sometimes it is so easy to get caught up in important tasks that the needs of important people are not met. As I stared at that piece of paper, I could think of a number of ways I should have handled the situation. The manner in which I had dealt with his place of peace had taken from him the one thing I had no right to remove: his optimism and hope for the future. I had forgotten that it wasn't just me who was relocating—he was trying to find a new home as well. With this insight, I retraced my steps and symbolically attempted to restore Jacob's place of peace. With a little time and patience, I removed the dangerous items without destroying his security.

Many years earlier, an event occurred which connects to Jacob's experience. When my wife Arlene was nine years old, her mother passed away. For one week she was surrounded by loving family, neighbors, and ward members. Their attention was suddenly torn away from her with the assassination of President John F. Kennedy. Everyone's focus was turned to their television sets, as a nation mourned together, and a little girl was left to mourn alone. In one week, she had lost the leader of her home, as well as the leader of her country. This would have been difficult at any age—what a challenge at the tender age of nine! It could well be asked, "Where was her place of peace?" She was almost the same age as Jacob was when he was looking for a place of peace in his new surroundings. His mother was looking for the same basic thing at a different time in a different set of circumstances.

My wife related that she felt there was no one to really turn to in her darkest hour. Everyone else seemed to be involved in their own level of grieving. So she knelt next to her bed and poured out her heart with expressions such as, "Why has this happened?" and "What will happen in the future?"

As she retold this experience to me, she simply said, "I was overwhelmed with a peace and a calm that gave me the feeling that He knew who I was and was aware of my circumstances." She added, "This feeling has remained with me throughout my life."

As I sit down to write these words, Jacob is in Calgary, Canada, serving a full-time mission. As a young boy, he correctly looked for a place of peace within his home. Presently, he is finding out that real peace can always be found in the same place no matter where you are. Actually, it is not found in a place, it is found in a person. That individual is the Savior! As my son has absorbed himself in the work of the Lord, he has discovered the real place of peace.

In a world where nations are quickly losing a desire for peace, individuals cry out to a greater degree for that security that can only be found in the Savior. When Christ comes again, every knee will bow in recognition that in Him is found the only place of peace. However, we do not need to wait until His Second Coming to gain that witness.

Elder Robert D. Hales said,

> As we look into the eyes of our children and grandchildren, we see the doubt and fear of our times. Wherever these precious ones go in the world, they hear about unemployment, poverty, war, immorality, and crime. They wonder, "How can we cope with these problems?"
>
> To find answers, they look back into our eyes and listen to our words. Do they hear us speaking faithfully and hopefully, despite the tribulations of our times? . . . When they see our steadfastness in keeping the commandments, their fears will subside and their confidence in the Lord will increase.

> By showing our faith through tribulation, we assure them that the fury of the adversary is not fatal. . . . My brothers and sisters, however dark conditions may seem in this world today, whatever the storms we are facing personally, in our homes and our families, this joy can be ours now. . . . The One who had power to calm the elements of earth has power to calm our souls, to give us refuge from the storm: "Peace, be still" (Mark 4:39).[26]

As we digest all the reassuring promises given to us individually and as a Church regarding the last days, it seems to me that the Brethren are trying to instill optimism in our hearts. The Gospel allows us to have the kind of composure in these tough times that will keep us from running around like Chicken Little, declaring "the sky is falling." Without an understanding of the promises to the faithful, we can easily overextend our stride, not in the work of the Lord, but in panic. The result being that spiritually, physically, and emotionally, we do have a hernia.

Notes

1. Jeffrey R. Holland, CES Fireside for Young Adults, Sept. 2004, BYU.
2. Orson Pratt, *Journal of Discourses,* 26 vols. (London: Latter-day Saints' Book Depot, 1865) 12:344; italics added)
3. See *Discourses of President Gordon B. Hinckley,* Vol. 2 (Salt Lake, Utah: The Church of Jesus Christ of Latter-day Saints, 2005) 523–24.
4. Gordon B. Hinckley, "If Ye Are Prepared Ye Shall Not Fear," *Ensign*, Nov. 2005, 61–62.
5. Harold B. Lee, *Ye Are the Light of the World* (Salt Lake City, Utah: Deseret Book, 1974), 350–51; italics added.
6. Ezra Taft Benson, *The Constitution: A Heavenly Banner* (Salt Lake City: Deseret Book, 1986), 32–33; italics added.)
7. Mark E. Peterson, *BYU Speeches of the Year* (Provo, Utah: Brigham Young University Press, 1968).
8. Ezra Taft Benson, *This Nation Shall Endure* (Salt Lake City: Deseret Book, 1977), 145.
9. Ezra Taft Benson, in Conference Report, Apr. 1962, 104; italics added.)
10. Dallin H. Oaks, "Bible Stories and Personal Protection," *Ensign*, Nov. 1992, 39–40.

11. Robert D. Hales, Faith through Tribulation Brings Peace and Joy, *Ensign*, May 2003, 16; italics added.
12. Wilford Woodruff, *Millennial Star*, 53:642–43, as quoted in Conference Report, Oct. 1982, 64.
13. Brigham Young, *Journal of Discourses*, 8:172; italics added.
14. Brigham Young, *Journal of Discourses*, 2:55.
15. Parley P. Pratt, as quoted by Matthew J. Grow, "The Extraordinary Life of Parley P. Pratt," *Ensign*, Apr. 2007, 56.
16. Gordon B. Hinckley, in Conference Report, Oct. 1982, 64; italics added.
17. Jeffrey R. Holland, "The Ministy of Angels," *Ensign*, Nov. 2008, 29–31.
18. Paul H. Dunn, "The Cheering Section," *Ensign*, June 1980, 4.
19. Brigahm Young, *Journal of Discourses*, 11:14; italics added.
20. Wilford Woodruff, *Discourses of Wilford Woodruff*, ed. by Homer Durham (Salt Lake City, Utah: Bookcraft, 1946), 230.
21. Jeffrey R. Holland, *However Long and Hard the Road* (Salt Lake City: Deseret Book, 1985), 13–14.
22. Neal A. Maxwell, *One More Strain of Praise* (Salt Lake City: Bookcraft, 1999), 11.
23. Ezra Taft Benson, "Spencer W. Kimball: A Star of the First Magnitude" *Ensign*, Dec. 1985, 33.
24. Jeffrey R. Holland, CES Fireside for Young Adults, Sept. 2004, BYU.
25. Dallin H. Oaks, "Bible Stories and Personal Protection," *Ensign*, Nov. 1992, 39.
26. Robert D. Hales, "Faith through Tribulation Brings Peace and Joy," *Ensign*, May 2003, 16–18.

chapter seven

Lengthen Your Stride without Getting a Hernia

MANY YEARS AGO I HAD AN ENLIGHTENING CONVERSATION with one of my students. He was a very sharp and sober-minded young man in his mid-twenties. He shared with me this personal observation: "In my early years growing up in the Church, I had a perception that if I kept myself worthy I would automatically recognize the promptings from the Holy Ghost. I believed that by serving a worthy mission and by being married properly in the temple I would understand the workings of the Spirit better than I do. But sometimes I really don't know the difference between my own thoughts and the promptings of the Spirit."

My immediate response was to reinforce that worthiness is merely the foundation in gaining a relationship with the Spirit. His misunderstanding regarding the companionship of the Spirit came from the fact that he did not see that his personal responsibility extended beyond just being clean.

I referred him to the Book of Mormon prophet Jacob, who was preparing to teach the allegory of Zenos when he stated, "I will unfold this mystery unto you; if I do not, by any means, *get shaken from my firmness in the Spirit*, and stumble *because of my over anxiety*" (Jacob 4:18; italics added.) Here was a prophet in the temple preaching the doctrines of the kingdom, and he was concerned about losing the Spirit over something as simple as anxiety. Even in his role as prophet, Jacob could not be in tune to the promptings of the Spirit if anxiety was a part of his life.

I asked my friend if he had adopted any negative attitudes or emotions that although they may not be sins in and of themselves, still might cause him to be insensitive to the whisperings of the still small voice. We reviewed a number of the circumstances and adverse emotions that might distance him from the Spirit. He was surprised to learn that things such as stress from the relentless demands of the clock, pressures to compete, fear of failure, academic demands, excessive workload, and many other things all had distanced him from recognizing the whisperings of the still small voice.

Over the years I have observed that his feelings are not uncommon, especially among returned missionaries. In fact, I would go so far as to say it is often a part of the normal maturing process in spiritual growth. The following are a few more attitudes or feelings that may not be sins, yet they distance us from the Spirit:

- Depression
- Worry
- Fear
- Lack of balance in priorities
- Insecurity
- Doubt
- Loneliness
- Resentment
- Tension
- Panic
- Irritability
- Frustration
- Defeat
- Despair
- Futility
- Grief
- Confusion

Gradually, he began to see that he had been under the false assumption that his sole responsibility was to avoid major sin so the Holy Ghost would naturally integrate itself into his life. I tried to help him understand that it takes more than being repulsed by sin, we also need to be proactive toward the Spirit even down to the very pace of our lives. Only then can we trust that our feelings are in tune with the Holy Ghost.

To illustrate this idea of pace, my student and I looked at a portion of King Benjamin's marvelous discourse to the Nephites in the latter stages of his life. He gave them a key to traveling through life at a pace that would allow the Spirit to be their companion: "And see that all these things are done in wisdom and order; for it is not requisite that a man should run faster than he has strength. And again, it is expedient that he should be diligent, that thereby he might win the prize; therefore, all things must be done in order" (Mosiah 4:27).

We gave special attention to the dynamics of what this prophet was saying to the Nephites, as well as to ourselves. It was not enough for my friend to do what was right, he also needed to conduct his life at a pace that was "diligent" and at the same time did not cause him to "run faster than he [had] strength."

There is a pace to living that allows the Lord to be our guide as we keep the commandments. It is ironic to me that so many of us answer the temple recommend questions in a positive way to be worthy to enter the temple, yet the very pace of our lives distances us from the daily companionship of that Spirit we so desire. This was certainly true of my young friend. I used King Benjamin's words to remind him that life's race is not a sprint but a long-distance run. Unlike a sprinter, a long distance runner must be mindful of a pace that allows him to finish strong, or, as the scriptures say, "endure unto the end" (1 Nephi 13:37).

I shared with him the Lord's counsel to Joseph Smith following the loss of the 116-page manuscript: "Do not run faster or labor more than you have strength" (D&C 10:4).

My young friend responded, "What about President Spencer W. Kimball's encouragement to 'lengthen our stride'?"

I reminded him that even a long-distance runner must lengthen his stride; he just doesn't do it so early in the race that he has no second wind and thus exhausts himself. We opened the New Testament and read, "Let us run with *patience* the race that is set before us" (Hebrews 12; italics added). I reviewed with him that patience is not required in a sprint. I informed him that if he were to continue his life at its present pace, he could have problems when he was older. I reminded him that it is very difficult to perform well in a long distance race when we begin our finishing kick too early in the race. While we must always be concerned with worthiness, we must also be aware of pace.

I asked him to join me in the basketball gym so I could make a point regarding this idea of spiritual pace. I stood on the baseline under the basket and had him do the same on the opposite end of the court under the opposing basket. I then had him sprint from where he was to the baseline where I was standing. I asked him to give his very best effort, to which he complied. I recorded the time of his mad dash using a stopwatch. Next, I had him repeat the procedure with one notable exception—this time he was to try to run just as fast as he had before, while at the same time dribbling a basketball.

The first few attempts ended when he lost control of the ball by "running faster than he was able" to maintain his companionship with the basketball. He had to repeat the sprint a few times in order to complete the task. As hard as he tried in his efforts at dribbling the ball, he was not able to duplicate his time recorded on his first sprint without the ball.

I reviewed with him the fact that his desire for speed rather than control was not only the cause of his losing the ball, but also possibly the cause of his lack of oneness with the Holy Ghost. Speed at the expense of control is not a realistic goal in basketball or in life. I identified how the task of dribbling a ball down the court is made more difficult when there is an opposing team present, with the desire to strip the ball from him. In life this opposing team, led by Satan, is trying just as hard to strip us of the companionship of the Spirit.

This is easy to recognize by observing young players dribbling the ball. They rarely succeed in controlling the ball because they repeatedly try to shove it into the floor rather than master the art of control. There is an ideal rhythm in bouncing the ball off the floor. In a sense it is the ball that dictates the pace in which we master the art of dribbling across the floor. With head down, totally unaware of his surroundings, the ineffective dribbler tries to plow through the opposition. If he does not lose control of the ball on his own, the opposition will surely accomplish the task. I asked my friend if this was not a little like his approach to life. I reminded him that like the effective dribbler, we must be in control of ourselves in order to be at one with the Spirit. The ball has its own pace, and an effective player must conform to it, in order to have the ball as his companion. And in life, it is the individual who must conform to the Spirit, not the other way around.

We read these words of President Henry B. Eyring that were presented to the students of BYU: "[The still small voice] is so quiet that if you are noisy inside, you won't hear it."[1] What a challenge—to learn how to give 100 percent of our energies and at the same time conduct ourselves at a pace in which we can feel the whisperings of the still small voice. It is so easy to have an accelerated pace in life that leaves us both exhausted and inefficient. On another occasion President Eyring said, "Now, I testify it is a small voice. It whispers, not shouts."[2]

I'm not sure if I communicated with him as effectively as I had hoped, but at the very least, it was a good reminder of the need to be in control of the pace of life in order to be sensitive to the whisperings of the Holy Ghost. I am convinced that if Satan can't influence us to sin outright, the next best things he can do is fill our lives with so much clutter that he becomes our silent partner, so silent that too often we are unaware of his influence in speeding up the pace of our lives and camouflaging our priorities. This clutter is not just cars, houses, and adult toys, but the internal clutter identified by the Prophet Jacob as anxiety, which causes our internal motors to run too fast.

Let there be no misunderstanding about what I mean concerning pace. Someone can be completely still and be operating at a pace that is not in their own best interest due to the presence of the internal tension brought on by something as simple as anxiety. However, physical exertion without internal tension can be rejuvenating to the body, as well as the soul. But a soul full of the negative emotions listed in this chapter is always running too fast and is incapable of lengthening his stride without becoming emotionally and spiritually out of balance

I am reminded of the story of an elderly man who rested by the side of a much-traveled path. A much younger man stopped for a minute next to the old gentleman. In the course of conversation the younger man asked, "How has life in America changed most?"

The old man replied simply, "Speed." Pausing for a moment to think, he continued, "It's killing us. You have to make a part of your life in which you slow down. The world won't do it for you."

The wisdom of the old man reminds us of one of the great truths regarding the Holy Ghost: speed is not a worthy substitute for control. My young friend's pace was a reflection that the stride which is lengthened beyond control will eventually self-destruct into a hernia.

In 1965 Virgil I. Grissom became the first astronaut to maneuver a spacecraft while orbiting the earth. He returned with a great lesson that slowing down actually places us further ahead. Regarding his experience in space, he said:

> "You can't just step on the gas out there. . . . In fact, one craft gains on another by slowing down." He explained that a decrease in speed

brings the craft closer to the earth. The orbit is thus shortened, and the craft gains by "riding closer to the rail [of gravity]."

Gus Grissom talked of space travel. He could have described how to get ahead on earth, too. Many a man moves out front by slowing down and putting better personal control on his course in life, even as Grissom skillfully maneuvered in orbiting.[3]

The Wisdom of the Feed Store Owner

For reasons I can't explain, I have never been comfortable in the city. I'm fine going to work or even visiting the city because I know I will be coming home soon. But staying too long anyplace where I am surrounded solely by the handiwork of man—the freeways, buildings, glass, and steel, give me a sense of claustrophobia. As I drive home from the urban valley where I work into the rural valley where I live, my spirit seems to breathe a great big sigh, which reaffirms, "I am where I need to be." It seems to have been that way from the day I was born.

I have consistently had the need for open spaces and animals. It is odd that this has always been a part of me, because my family never had land, horses, or any kind of open range. As a boy I loved westerns, not just because of the stories, but because I could usually count on the beautiful scenery that accompanied those wide open spaces shown on the movie screen. To the aggravation of many people, I used to give a fairly decent John Wayne impression at every opportunity. It became such a part of me that for a while my friends called me Duke.

A few years after my wife and I were married, an opportunity to live in a small house surrounded by horses lazily grazing on pasture land made itself available. The decision to move in was about as difficult as a hungry child wishing for a "happy meal" at McDonalds. We loved it so much; but there is a big difference between watching westerns on the big screen and taking care of horses and pasture land.

One of my first problems were the weeds—not all the weeds, just one particular kind. All the spraying I did seemed to have no effect on those unwelcome intruders. To make matters worse, the horses would not graze in the area inhabited by those green pests. So I went to the local feed store and asked the man behind the counter what I should do. He looked at me with a sly smile and picked up a product he seemed to have full faith in. As he handed the bottle to me, he said in a voice of soft confidence, "This will solve the problem."

With complete faith in his quiet confidence, I sprayed the pasture. For good measure, I went over it twice. Too my surprise, the weed killer not only didn't kill the weeds, it seemed to act like a fertilizer. Feeling a bit ripped off, I went back to the man and sarcastically reported that the weeds were doing better than ever. He asked me how long it had been since I sprayed the field. I responded that it had only been a few days.

I reminded him that how long ago I sprayed was not the issue. The point I was trying to make was that the weeds were not just living—they were thriving. All of this had occurred after spraying the pasture with the product he sold me. Reassuring me that "patience was a virtue," he told me to wait a few more days for the results he promised.

Sure enough, within a couple of days the weeds no longer looked in the prime of life. And it was not long after that, that they simply withered and died.

Overjoyed, I returned to the store owner to share the good news. Following my report, I inquired, "How did that stuff work?"

He replied, "Well, first of all, the product I sold you was not a weed killer." He continued, "It was a steroid. It caused the weeds to grow so fast they actually committed suicide."

Over the years I have had the opportunity to ponder his words. I have come to the conclusion that growing or moving too fast can cause the basic framework that holds societies together to commit a similar kind of suicide. As a boy I remember hearing some elderly people in my small town lament that the changes brought on by planes and cars caused family members to live farther apart. Their conclusion was that while they enjoyed these conveniences, this had caused them to lose contact with those they grew up with. It seemed as if they were saying that "in moving fast we have moved too far away from those we love." I could not image a world without these advances, so their words to me seemed a bit out of touch. To my young mind their words bore witness that time had passed them by.

I suppose today I am feeling some of the same angst as these elderly people of my youth. With all the wonders of the Internet, cell phones, and technology that bless our lives, I can't help worrying that we are moving too fast. Surface-level technological contact will never be an adequate substitute for face-to-face interaction. I fear the long range implications of being able to connect with people in ways that engage the intellect without fully embracing the entire person. I fear that we may be trading our desire to build our relationships with technological speed. Our youth must be careful to not allow technology to move them so quickly through their relationships that they don't take the time to sink their roots deeply into the type of soil that can only be nourished with time and face-to-face interaction. Recently, we had a gathering of family for Thanksgiving. With all kinds of time to talk face-to-face, play games, or have fun outside, the teenagers eventually migrated to a quiet room to spend time on their laptops. While they were in the same room, there was very little interacting with each other. It seemed as if technology had made them socially retarded in their ability to listen and speak face-to-face.

The wisdom of the feed store owner echoes through today's world. Could these wonderful advances in technology be a kind of steroid? Are they causing us to grow so fast as a society that we actually may be committing suicide? The implications are obvious: If we are not careful, we just might lengthen our stride to the point of having a disastrous hernia. Individuals as well as nations must realize "speed is never a worthy substitute for control."

I Choose Not to Have Stress

It seems almost comical to me that when I am introduced at speaking engagements, it is customary to mention the academic degrees that I have obtained. What many people don't realize is that (at least for me) obtaining these degrees had much less to do with my intelligence and more with my persistence. It was not uncommon in the years I was in school to find myself somewhere between "completely lost" and "totally overwhelmed." This also included the twelve years of education before college. It would not be an understatement to say that no one was more surprised than me that I obtained a PhD. While I enjoyed my years at Shasta College, Brigham Young University, and the University of New Mexico, I often felt out of place in the environment of higher education.

This was the era in which almost all the exams were taken in class rather than at a testing center. It didn't take me long to realize that I was the last one finished on almost all of those testing occasions. It got to the point that I was more interested in completing the exam with speed than with accuracy. It should not have taken me too much pondering to recognize that I was missing the point. But anxiety moves even normal people to totally irrational behavior. During those times of testing, my anxiety level was such that at certain moments it felt like I was going to pass out.

Each occasion in which I walked up to the teacher's desk as the last one to finish, I somehow felt that my stupidity was being validated in the presence of my peers. On those occasions, how I did on the exam wasn't nearly as important to me as the fact that I was once again making that long walk to the teacher's desk as the last one finished. In that mind-set I was more than willing to "substitute speed for control."

While attending Brigham Young University, I developed a strategy designed to ease my tremendous test anxiety. I went to some of my professors and asked if I could take their exams in the waiting area near their offices. After explaining my reasons, I indicated that I would sit in full view of their secretaries and would even be willing to take the exams early. I was ready to do anything to avoid the tremendous anxiety brought on by my feelings of insecurity. To my surprise a number of my teachers compassionately consented to my request.

The days, weeks, and months wove together, and over time, I completed my bachelor's degree at BYU. At that point I didn't feel a sense of accomplishment as much as a tremendous relief that I had somehow dodged a bullet. I joyfully accepted the opportunity to teach seminary in Phoenix, Arizona. For a number of years, my family and I lived in the warm bliss of the Valley of the Sun. However, it became obvious that we could not continue to work for the Church at the level of pay that was offered for a bachelor's degree. So we made the painful break from our life in Arizona and traveled back to Utah for me to obtain a master's degree. It did not take long for my academic insecurities to surface once more.

Even though I was in my mid-thirties, nothing had emotionally changed for me in the classroom. In my heart, I was still that insecure boy in kindergarten that needed his mother to almost coax him through the school door each day. That's the funny thing about fearful things—they don't have to be rational, and when the elements that first created the fear are present, the individual is often reduced (at an emotional level) to the age when the fears began. I never identified when mine began, they just always seemed to be a part of my educational experience. I have a dear friend who has a PhD and is a successful husband and father as well as a leader in the Church. But he has a phobia that began in his youth regarding clowns. He is absolutely hilarious when he shares his experiences with clowns, from his childhood as well as his adult life. One afternoon I was visiting in his office when I flippantly made the observation that surely he wasn't afraid of clowns anymore. In an almost apologetic fashion, he replied that the seeds of fear were still there, and he would not go out of his way to be in the presence of a person dressed as a clown. At that moment, I realized that being a student in school was for me like being in the presence of a person dressed as a clown for him.

I didn't have problems with the papers to be written or even the oral presentations in front of the class. I didn't even have many problems with the take-home exams. But for reasons I have never identified, my fears regarding in-class testing had not changed a single bit. Each time I was placed in that environment, I just had to white knuckle my way through it.

As I progressed through my master's experience, a very dark cloud waited for me on the horizon. Unlike my bachelor's degree, in order to complete my master's degree, I would have to complete a comprehensive written exam as well as an oral exam at the conclusion of my course work. I was not worried about the oral exam, but my fears concerning the written exam grew like a quiet cancer as the day drew nearer.

Those who have the "shadow on the brain" brought on by fear are no strangers to procrastination. Sure enough, when I completed my course work, instead of just going in to take the exam, I devised a plan that was really just a cover-up for my anxious fears. I decided I needed a full semester to prepare for my finals. So I took a summer break from work and took out a loan that would take care of our financial needs for the semester. I went to each one of my teachers and asked them the areas I should focus on in my preparation for the comprehensive final exam. Following a thorough review of my class notes, tests, and text books, I wrote the questions (as well as the answers) that might be asked on the exam. I placed the questions on one side of a 3x5 card and the answers on the flip-side. When I completed this part of my preparation, I was left with quite a stack of 3x5 cards.

Following this, I arose each morning and walked for the entire day while I studied. Because of my nervousness, I found it helpful to walk rather than sit at a desk and study my notes. I followed the ritual of reading a question and then answering it aloud. I then turned over the card and read the answer to see if I was correct. I found that it took nearly an entire work day to successfully go through the cards a couple of times. This was the daily format I followed five to six days per week. Looking back on it now, I'm sure I was completely prepared to take the exam months before the date arrived. However, when a person is filled with anxiety, they never know when their brain will turn to oatmeal, and the information will be lost from their minds like data being erased from a computer. Nothing suffers like a person's memory in the presence of anxiety.

The night before the exam I stayed alone in a little bedroom, which was just behind our home. I didn't want to keep my wife awake as I suffered with my fears regarding the next day. Study seemed to be a wasted venture as my anxiety overwhelmed my ability to focus. Sleep was just as difficult for the same reasons. In my exhaustion, I collapsed on the bed for some much needed rest. I don't know how long I was asleep, but something happened that I will always accept as a gift from the Lord.

I awoke a few hours after falling asleep. The anxiety that made it so difficult to sleep was totally removed. I was immediately aware of the complete calm that engulfed me from the inside out. What a contrast to the fearful anxiety that was such a part of me prior to that moment.

Words came into my heart with such penetrating force that I wrote them down: "Stress is not an event. It is a reaction to an event. It is a choice. You can choose not to have stress."

That was a revelation to me. There is no question in my mind regarding the matter. I quickly grabbed a 3x5 card and wrote down the words. This was not an impression—these were actual words that came into my heart with such clarity it was as if I were hearing them.

The calmness did not leave me for an extended period of time during the night. Then, as quickly as it came, the peaceful security of the Spirit left me to myself. Periodically, through the rest of the night and the following morning of the exam, I had bouts of jolting anxiety. I confidently repeated these words which empowered me in my battle with my fears: "I choose not to have stress!"

As I said the words, I was reminded of the reality of what had happened in the night. A portion of the peace I had felt returned to me long enough for me to relax and more forward. As I walked into the department office to take the written exam, I was as comfortable as if I had already successfully completed the test. I had prepared to the best of my abilities, and I knew it. Even more important, I knew my Heavenly Father knew it. Because of this and what had happened the previous night, I had faith that all would be well.

As I remember it, we were given four hours to complete the final. I was finished within an hour and thirty minutes. How odd that was compared with my previous experiences with testing. As I walked out of the department office, I felt a peace and a calm that I had not expected. I had hoped and prayed for success for so long, I thought that I would be jumping for joy. Somehow that just didn't seem to be important at that point. What I thought was going to be an exam proved to be something much more. My Heavenly Father chose this occasion to teach me something greater than academics. With His help, I could face my fears and walk through life with a confidence reflected in the knowledge that He would always be there—even in the midst of my fears.

Even though it has been many years since that experience, there have been many times I have repeated the phrase, "I choose not to have stress!" It has helped me in overcoming the crippling fear of failure and its companion anxiety. Repeating those words is like ripping the head off the bear suit to remind myself that I am the person inside. It has allowed me to move forward, lengthening my stride, without the fear of overwhelming or overextending myself. After all, if the Savior has the power to calm the seas, why wouldn't He have the power to calm me? I testify on that night, He did just that.

Brigham Young said:

> The feeling of calmness and serenity . . . manifests faith in the Lord. . . . We should be perfectly calm and serene, . . . otherwise we will be excited . . . and thus shall not be able to act prudently and in a way that would be pleasing in the sight of our Father in heaven. Sailors and mariners become wise, useful, and qualified for their stations only by experience. Storms, tempests, and hurricanes have to occur in order to give them that experience. If all was calm, and storms never arose at sea, where would the mariner get the experience that is necessary for him to have.[4]

I believe the Lord was using the storms that raged during my experience with academics to teach me this principle.

Pace and Priorities

I am convinced that the lessons which impact us the most come from our own experience. From an intellectual standpoint, I knew what I was teaching my student regarding "speed and control" (at the beginning of this chapter) was true, but an experience I had shortly after our encounter branded it into my soul.

It was the weekend before a new school year. I had all the feelings of anxiety and of running faster than I should as a teacher. For some reason, the days just before a new school year have always been a very stressful time for me. It is a feeling similar to those times when I was a young athlete, just before a contest was about to begin. It didn't matter what the sport was, the anxiety I felt just before the event was always the same. It always felt like a near-lethal mixture of anxiety combined with fear and trembling. On a physical level, I'm sure I was going through all the negative toxins that result in the body of one who is constantly "calling out to the fire department when there is no fire." In a manner of speaking, I was about to experience the "hernia," the gift we give to ourselves when we have lengthened our stride to the point of running too fast.

On that particular day, this combination of emotions nearly became lethal for me as I was hurrying down the hallway just outside my classroom. As quickly as turning off a light switch, I suffered a heart attack that caused me to crumple to the floor. It was as if I had been unplugged from the power source that had kept me going for decades. This was the first of three heart attacks I have had over the past eleven years. I guess I'm either going to perfect the art of having heart attacks or I'm going to perfect the art of stopping them. As difficult as it has been, the lessons I have taken from it has been spiritually compensating.

As my energy suddenly came to a halt, it seemed that the energy level of everyone in close proximity increased. With everything happening so fast around me, I felt like a spectator at an event that was of paramount importance to me but one in which I was not allowed to participate. I felt like a fish in an aquarium, watching others work all around me yet I was unable to do anything except observe. My body had suddenly become so weak that it took all of my strength just to bring forth a whisper. Fearing that I might lose even that ability, I remained completely silent. Lying as still as possible, I placed my fate in the hands of trained professionals as well as the Lord.

It is amazing how the events of life change so quickly. One moment, I was walking down the hallway; the next, I was waking up in a hospital bed a number of hours after a medical procedure that had required major anesthesia. All of this had taken almost a full day. How can something feel like it transpired in an instant and an eternity at the same time? The physical pace of my life had come to an abrupt halt. My to-do list had suddenly been wiped clean.

Still not knowing what had gone wrong with me physically, I awoke in great pain, accompanied by feelings of tremendous despair and anxiety. For some reason, there was nothing they could give me that would remove, or even dull, these monumental feelings.

This was early Sunday morning and the doctor who had been working on me hustled into the room on his morning rounds. After a few minutes of conversation with my wife, he stepped toward the door. Almost as an afterthought, he turned to me and said, "Oh, you've had a heart attack. I'll be back later in the evening to discuss it with you."

A number of my relatives, including my father, had died very young of heart attacks or strokes. The doctor's words brought me to the shocking realization of my own mortality. As he walked through the doorway and moved briskly in the direction of the next item on his list of things to do, I interrupted his exit by appealing, "Can't we take a minute now and talk about this?"

He looked at me with eyes that seemed to have a firm focus on personal priorities. No longer referring to me as a patient but as a member of the Church, he said, "Brother Bassett, I am surprised at you. This is Sunday; you know that I am a bishop and that I have council meetings to attend to before sacrament meeting." Following this gentle chiding, he continued, "I'll see you later tonight." Without waiting for a reply, he exited the room.

As I lay there alone in the midst of my despair, my heart cried out, "Am I not more important than a meeting? Aren't people more important than meetings?"

Even in the midst of my self-pity, I was fully aware that my doctor was a good man and a dedicated bishop. He had no intention of hurting me; in fact, his only goal was to aid me in my recovery. His plate was just overflowing with people who needed his time professionally and ecclesiastically. He did not have the time to meet the needs of all the people who demanded his attention. Still, I felt there was a lesson for me to learn in the experience.

How I wished that I could go back and meet the needs of those I had unknowingly passed by because I had been running too fast to be sensitive to their needs. As I lay there in that bed, my mind raced back through the years to all those who had been in the position of need I was currently in—perhaps not physically but emotionally or spiritually. But just as this doctor was unaware of my feelings at that time, I too was not aware of those I had dealt with in this manner. I had been so caught up in my own list of things to do that I wondered how many people, students, neighbors, and even family members had come to me in pain and despair and left with the feeling that a meeting, or someone else, or maybe just my own time was more important to me than they were.

My frustration lay in the fact that I had been guilty of the same thing so many times and in so many positions of service over the years. I was reminded, once again, that quite often we don't see the world as it is; we see the world as we are. I had now come eye to eye with someone just like me, and I did not enjoy the view.

Elder Neal A. Maxwell wrote, "Imperviousness to the promptings of the still small voice of God will . . . mean that we have ears, but cannot hear, not only the promptings of God but also the pleas of men."[5] I pondered the pace of my own service. Had I been sensitive to "the promptings of the still small voice" and "the pleas of men" as I needed to be? Now this heart attack had suddenly wiped my planner clean, and I was left to ponder how I wanted to conduct myself when I got back on my feet. Certainly, my decision for the future was not to cancel or avoid all meetings but to use those meetings more profitably and not to schedule so many of them that the needs of the very people I was trying to serve became secondary. I made a commitment to myself that I would make every attempt to avoid getting so caught up in my activities, programs, and meetings that I might fail to respond to a suffering soul whose only need may be a listening ear.

I knew it was vitally important that when I got back on my feet, I needed to conduct my life at a pace that would allow me to respond appropriately to the promptings of the Spirit. I was aware that pace must always be aware of priorities.

I read once that we all recognize a fool when we see one, but we rarely recognize a fool when we are one. It is odd how it took a doctor whose behavior was just like mine for me to recognize a change needed to take place in me.

No Tension—No Scarring

When our skin is painfully cut there is a natural healing process that takes over. The end result of this process is a scar, and it becomes a part of us from that day forward. Have you ever wondered why scar tissue does not form when a plastic surgeon does the cutting?

> The answer is that if you cut your face and it "heals naturally," scar tissue will form, because there is a certain amount of tension in the wound and just underneath the wound which pulls the surface of the

> skin back, creates a "gap" so to speak, which is filled in by scar tissue. When a plastic surgeon operates, he not only pulls the skin together closely by sutures, he also cuts out a small amount of flesh underneath the skin so that *there is no tension present*. The incision heals smoothly, evenly, and with no distorting surface scar.[6]

What a fascinating conclusion that when no tension is present there can be no scarring. I am absolutely convinced the same principle is true in our lives. I mentioned earlier in this chapter that it is possible to honestly answer all the temple recommend questions to obtain a recommend, while at the same time not having the companionship of the Holy Ghost. You learned that the internal pace of our lives can distance us from the promptings of the Spirit. I believe the elements that cause us to run so fast and to lose touch with the still small voice, are part of this tension, which leads to a kind of a spiritual scarring. When we are truly at peace in our worthiness, as well as our pace and priorities, there will be no tension. The result will be that we will have the power to accept all that life has to offer without scarring.[7]

CONCLUSION

At this point in my life, I have discovered that as I focus on the positive and view my surroundings with optimism, my health is returning to me, and I can feel my own stride beginning to lengthen. I must admit my motives in writing this book have been somewhat self-serving. This book has truly been written as a self-help book. The self I was trying to help was me. In the process, I have been more successful in fighting off fear, anxiety, depression, and the host of other negative emotions that often come as a natural result of trauma.

A dear friend of mine in her eighties, named Muriel Cox, went to bed one night feeling as normal as ever. In the morning she awoke to discover that she was blind. She has been that way for the past two years. I have been inspired by her optimistic courage. Almost as an afterthought, one evening she said, "I'm just playing the cards I've been dealt." Each time I have visited with her, it is I who has been comforted and left her home recommitted to do a better job "playing the cards I've been dealt."

She also concluded our visit one time with this thought: "Blindness is not for sissies." That is the closest thing to self-pity she has ever expressed to me.

She shared something else which captured a bright aspect to the process of enduring to the end: "At this point in my life, I know I won't go to the grave in a pretty body. But I plan on sliding into the grave like I've just hit an inside-the-park home run and scream at the top of my lungs, 'Wow what a ride!' "

She is a perfect reflection of someone who is dealing with the "real bears" of life. I invite you, the reader, to categorize the bears in your life. If they are real, then deal with them with enthusiastic optimism and faith. If they are creations of your own imagination, or "men in bear suits," rip their heads off to discover that you are the one inside.

In the days ahead of us we have been told to expect a great deal of war and economic difficulties. As we focus on the reassuring promises given by the Lord's servants, we will be blessed with a peace that will allow us to endure well.

The pace of our lives is a reflection of our values as well as our faith. Let us appropriately lengthen our stride, allowing us to productively live well all the days of our lives.

In this book I have attempted to state those things that I am holding on to in the hope that I can deal with the "bears" in my own life. It is my deepest hope that the journey through these pages will empower you to do the same. I would remind you that we don't have to get sick in order to get better.

The past eleven years of my life, I have had to deal with the kind of trauma that I had previously believed would happen at the last moment of a person's life. It seems in order for me to grow up spiritually, the Lord has allowed me to quickly grow old physically. Twelve years ago, it felt like I was blessed with a forever case of "Peter Pan Disease." My body felt like it would be forever young. It appeared that I was to be one of the "blessed ones" who would be strong and stand tall well into old age.

The emotions which have accompanied this new lifestyle have shifted my self-concept from one who is strong and confident physically, to one who is fragile and dependent on the Lord to a greater degree. I have discovered that as my physical strength has been challenged, I have had to make a decision to be bitter or to be better. A person who loses one of the physical senses often discovers that other senses have become more acute. What I have lost physically the past eleven years has given me a greater awareness of my spiritual senses. This has been a generous compensating blessing.

I have been invited to spend less time competing and more time serving, less time comparing and more time noticing the good in other people, less time climbing ladders of success and more time simply being still. I have discovered as I have focused on the elements of emotional control rather than worldly accomplishment, my world has changed from one of challenge to one of beauty—from one of personal power to one of personal peace. My need to categorize people is being replaced with the joy of accepting diversity.

My friendship with Muriel Cox has led me to believe that the secret of success is understanding that lengthening our stride is not really physical, it is spiritual. Her ability to do many things physically has diminished over time, but her spiritual stride has lengthened to championship levels. Time may slow each of us down physically, but spiritually lengthening our stride will give us a second wind, which may empower our bodies to a new season of "selective productivity." As the years add up, the events of our lives will stretch each of us to the point of having a "hernia" if we do not embrace this truth. My deepest hope is that the reader may recognize that "lengthening our stride" is not a goal; it is a gift that comes naturally to those whose attitudes and conduct approximate the Savior's.

During the four month season of healing at home, I have been writing this text for a few hours each day. This process has truly been a blessing for me and has been a part of my recovery. I will go back to work and face my own bears. I will discover if I can practice the counsel I have placed in these pages. I have come to the conclusion that the Lord will determine when it is time for me to return home—but for now it is I who must dictate the pace and attitude that will accompany me as I resume my teaching and my life. I thank you, the reader, for allowing me to be as personal as I have been in this book. I genuinely hope the journey has helped you lengthen your own stride and incorporate the positive lean that is common among those who are blessed with the spirit of optimism.

Notes

1. Henry B. Eyring, *Devotional and Fireside Speeches, 1988-1989,* 16.
2. Henry B. Eyring, "To Draw Closer to God," *Ensign*, May 1991, 67.
3. Wendell J. Ashton, *To Thine Own Self* (Salt Lake City: Bookcraft, 1972) 50.

4. *Journal of Discourses*, 5:322.
5. Neal A. Maxwell, *A Time to Choose* (Salt Lake City: Deseret Book, 1972), 59–60, 71.
6. Maxwel Maltz, *Psycho-Cybernetics* (New York: Prentice-Hall, 1960), 143; italics added.
7. For a further treatment of this subject see *Life Lessons From The Book of Mormon,* Christianson and Bassett (Springville, UT: Cedar Fort, 2008), 187–200, as well as *The Barber's Song,* Bassett (Springville, UT: Cedar Fort, 2005), 123–136.

about the author

K. Douglas Bassett completed a bachelor's degree as well as a master's degree from Brigham Young University. He earned his PhD from the University of New Mexico. He taught seminary for many years in Arizona, California, and Utah. He has also taught religion classes at BYU. He is currently teaching at the Orem Institute of Religion. All totaled, he has been involved in teaching for the Church Education system for thirty years.

Doug has written many books, including *The Barber's Songs, Life Lessons from the Book of Mormon,* and *Doctrinal Insights to the Book of Mormon.*

He and his wife, the former Arlen Chapman, live in Mona, Utah. They are the parents of eight children as well as four grandchildren.

0 26575 52910 4